MW01118679

my

proposal:

nothing

but

a

gracechild

my
proposal:

nothing
but
a
gracechild

REVELATIONS OF A PRODIGAL SON
NOW IN GOD-CAUSED EXILE

spirit of Moses

GRACECHILD
PUBLISHING
MARYLAND 2004

GRACECHILD PUBLISHING
A Division of Bethesda Nu'ahch Ministry Enterprises (bnME), LLC.
Greenbelt MD 20768

This book contains works of fiction in the form of short stories and poems. Any references to real people, events, establishments, organizations, or locales are intended only to give the fiction a sense of reality and authenticity. Other names, characters, and incidents are either the product of the author's imagination or are used completely fictitiously, as are those fictionalized events and incidents that involve real persons.

For information regarding special discounts for bulk purchases, contact Gracechild Publishing Special Sales: BNMEGRACECHILD@aol.com

Gracechild Publishing logo created by
Kendra (Keni) Williams of Pnuema Graphix

Printed in the United States of America

Designed by The Arden Charis Group

Cover, spine, "About the Author" and "The Foreknowledge" photographs by Greg Alexander

Back flap photograph courtesy Moses Thomas Alexander Greene

ISBN 0-9723081-0-5

To my father,
Moses,
the sure shot of my life. I lived a life of abundance because of what you were denied and denied yourself. Life shall never be the same because I live knowing "my daddy loves me unconditionally." You are my hero.

and to my mother,
Betty Faye,
who carries my name before the Lord each morning; whose ways of holiness, integrity and wisdom made way for this level of deliverance and resilience in me. I am still standing because you refused to give up on me. I rise and call you "Blessed".

and to my brother born for adversity,
Jerome Anthony,
who embodies the dogged determination of the four men who carried their paralyzed friend to Jesus on his sick bed. "Hey, bruddah." You interceded until you knew I knew "Jesus forgives sin." Thanks for teaching me to how to fight and how to "...having done all, stand." You are the best.

and to my pastor,
John K. Jenkins, Sr.,
a gift I could have never formed words to ask for but God knew I needed; without whose consistent wisdom and ways of excellence I would have never learned how to "run with the horses." You preached the word of God in love, with compassion, and through understanding and changed the direction of my life. The spirit of Moses is free because God used the spirit of John.

This book is also dedicated in honor of the grandparents of my life: Rose, Augustus Harvey, Mildred, Washington Wayman, Mary, Jesse, Ernest, Eliza, Sister Carey, Marjorie, and Thelma. I am today because of your choices.

THE INVITATION

In no way is this book a surface text. [1] To some, it may look like a collection of literary babbling and drunkenness; similar to the attributes given to Hannah as she poured out her soul before God for a male-child.

The revelation of being absolutely nothing but a gracechild came through much prayer, loss and pain; several seasons of tears, empty harvests and brokenness; the destructions of my own dreams, challenges to my ideologies and death of my identity; the raw numbness (almost like in waves) from being left by and having to leave behind Jonathan-David, countenance building, sweet counsel, "there for you when no one else was" friends; and God uprooting relationships I took too long to dissolve and being stricken with barrenness for bitterness I chose not to resolve. There was nothing grammatically, intellectually or religiously correct about the moments that birthed such revelations in me. I consciously, (with much prayer and a multitude of counselors), decided to stay as true as possible to those moments of my life so that you, as reader, would be a partaker of the same grace that I now walk in: God never blessed me for my perfection.

I invite you to identify with the performer and the minister parts of me. Performing has always been ministry for me. Always. I write like I speak and how I hear sound. 'gracechild is your invitation to become one with that voice, ear and creative process. For certain pieces, the only way that you will gain the full meaning of my offering, of the true emotion of that particular moment, will be to read this work aloud and then reflect.

---

[1] You are cordially invited to experience a book like you have never experienced one before.

I ask you to understand from the first read that I purposely, at times, write to cause a "mm?". Here is a primary example. I know that the correct spelling of the word "moment" is "m-o-m-e-n-t" but I spell it "moemeant." It is done on purpose. It is done to involve you in the text; that you would inwardly, emotionally, historically, Biblically, secularly, psychoanalytically, sociologically, experientially and actively dig deeper for answers to questions which you normally would not require of yourself.

Why would I purposely misspell the word "moemeant"? What is your name? Write it here. _____ Was there ever a time or season in your life that you intended to do one thing but found yourself doing another? (Read Romans 7 of the Holy Bible). What I am trying to communicate to you in spelling a common word this way is that there were times when I, (Moses), set out to do one thing, when I, (Mo-ses), <u>meant</u> holiness from the offset, onset, aboutset and going throughset but I, (Moe), missed the mark completely. In this text, I call it a "moemeant;" a time, when I (Moe-ses) meant to and had all intentions of meeting the requirements of the integrity within but gloriously missed. So to you as a reader, when you come upon the word "moemeant," I ask you not to look solely at the context of what you have just read, but rather, challenge **<u>yourself</u>** to ask **<u>yourself</u>** (if your name is Tyrone), what have been your "tymeants" or if your name is Louis, your "loumeants" or Aileen, your "ailmeants." (Then, go onto victory and realize that the blood of Jesus already cleanses you for your moemeants.) The hidden things in this text (once discovered) level the playing field.

And of punctuation marks, why would I leave errors? Perhaps, it is because you will identify with the fact that when engaged in intense dialogue, what mattered most was not where the period was placed or that the person took a breath for the comma or even said the correct things. In my relationship with Jehovah God, when I have a real need to bring before the presence of Him as my Father, I no longer seek to pray with all commas and periods in the right places and having all subjects and verbs agreeing. A Heaven and earth agreement has brought about more in my life versus that which pertains to proper grammar.

So, I welcome you to keep reading. The way 'gracechild has been written was the only way I knew to communicate my Hannah emotion, my Jesus in the Garden of Gethsemane anguish and many days which could best be expressed by groaning.

CONTENTS

(come)
FOREWORD

I n an age during which the prevailing themes of the Church of the Living God are "destiny," "purpose," and "wealth," it has become increasingly important to hear messages that remind us that in addition to each of these things, God is also now (and has always been) calling His people to holiness. In "my proposal: nothing but a gracechild", educator, music minister, actor, model, visionary and first-time author Moses T. Alexander Greene offers insight into a segment of his personal sanctification process towards this holiness. Not only does "spirit of Moses," (the author's pen name), overcome *his* adversary in this creatively written testimony, but the transparency of this text subtly challenges readers to be forthright with themselves such that they too experience Alexander Greene's level of inner freedom. The work seems to be Alexander Greene's hope that readers will naturally arrive at his same revelation: "i am nothing but a gracechild."

The very cover of the book mirrors the innocence, depth of thought, resilience and literary artistry through which the spirit of Moses communicates. Each chapter embraces brokenness and then releases it to us. Alexander Greene's transparency of struggle, anger, abandonment, habitual sin, bitterness and dependency of God alone are each brushstrokes that beautify his story, colorize his voice, and bring substance to our understanding.

However artistic, the book's greater poignancy is in its capacity to minister to those who can admit that somewhere in their lives they are less than perfect. As I read 'gracechild, I found that Alexander Greene confronted a problem that many Christians and just "plain-folk" in general, (regardless of their deity relationship) face. It is the unspoken yet universally understood requirement to daily present one image of ourselves to the world, however, when alone, have to deal directly with consequences of choices made outside of the will of God for our lives. These decisions always affect the spirit, soul, mind, body, and all aspects of a person's life. As an educator who taught decision making principles in the classroom for over a decade, to judge behavior (a series of decisions) Alexander Greene exhibited in his present, without examining, even if momentarily, factors of his childhood, adolescence development, and/or his feelings about his environment, would greatly impair anyone who wanted to receive the full ministry of this offering.

What further positions this book as a powerful ministry tool is the extent to which spirit of Moses continually beckons us to become a part of his experience and "get understanding." The acquisition of understanding seems to be an underlying theme of the book and purpose for his writing. Although there are certain messages that definitely seem to be camouflaged, to ensure that the reader receives *understanding* of a pivotal issue in his life, Moses T. Alexander Greene brings to the forefront his own sexual abuse.

There is nothing in the text that led me to believe that Alexander Greene introduced his sexual abuse, feelings of rejection or his relationship with members of his family as an excuse for his choices. Rather, spirit of Moses seems to be preparing the ground for deliverance by simply acknowledging that violation occurred. There were times when I wondered, "How many people would be *one day freer* if they were able to acknowledge the same?" Such honesty coming from a man is refreshing by itself. However, this same veracity coming from a twenty something, Christian, African-American man invigorated my soul and has the potential to empower a sea of minds to confront and tear down their own historical, spiritual and cultural strongholds.

Having been sexually molested at an early age without his parents' knowledge, spirit of Moses has had to, (as all persons who have been molested—whether sexually, mentally, emotionally, physically or spiritually—must), confront the demonic spirits that accompany and are imparted to the abused as a result of their experience(s) with the abuser. All acts of evil are performed in the physical realm; however, they are spiritual in nature because they directly affect a person's spirit, soul, mind, body, and all of his or her life.

All abused people must directly deal with the destructive agents that accompany every form of abuse. **TO NOT CONFRONT THE ABUSE (AND IN SOME CASES THE ABUSER) GIVES THE AGENTS OF DESTRUCTION LEGAL GROUND TO CONTINUALLY AFFECT THE PERSON AND HIS OR HER LIFE.** This holds true for not only for Moses T. Alexander Greene but **ANYONE WHO SUFFERED ABUSE**.

In pieces such as "Statutory Psalm" and "I Dream of Ichabod Webs" we see spirit of Moses attempting to understand his propensity for habitual sin. Of sin *behavior*, even if its roots were based in a violation such as molestation or rape, it must be dealt with. **SIN NOT DIRECTLY CONFRONTED GIVES BIRTH TO GENERATIONAL CURSES.** As roaches multiply if not combated so does sin until it contaminates and destroys everything and everyone within its path. Therefore, **SIN MUST BE CONFRONTED, CONFESSED, FORSAKEN, AND ABANDONED IN ORDER FOR A PERSON TO**

BECOME ALL THAT GOD DESTINED FOR THEM BEFORE THE FOUNDATIONS OF THE WORLD.

[No person is immune to sin; (by nature we are shaped in iniquity and born into an imperfect world). Satan's agenda and mandate have not changed. His main purpose remains to "kill, steal, and destroy." Whether Christian or not, all people have been and are being affected by Satan's devious, vile and hateful tactics against them and their lives. Furthermore, one's culture, social status, wealth, education, beauty, power or any other standard against which man measures himself successful cannot prevent Satan and his agents of destruction from attacking them in hopes of destroying them.

It is only the Word and the power of Jehovah God that can truly set the captive free. Only true confession and honesty of who we are in and outside of Jesus Christ can help us to walk into the divine destiny, purpose and true prosperity that God has for those that will before "the World" call upon Jesus as Lord and Savior of their lives. For it is not His will that any should perish, but that all should come to repentance.]

"my proposal: nothing but a gracechild" (the revelations of a prodigal son now in God-caused exile) is Moses T. Alexander Greene's personal inner confrontation and outward confession. It, however, is also encouragement for each one of us to look deep within ourselves to review those areas of our lives that cause us pain and sorrow and then confront and confess them.

My prayer for the author and all who read this book is: that,
1. Both look directly at themselves and make sure their lives line up with what God (not the Church) says they are and should become;

2. In their lives they will forsake all persons, agendas and mindsets that make them less than God's will says they are and should be;

3. Where there is brokenness, anger or bitterness for having been abused that they will ask and receive God's healing; or if they are an abuser, that they will simply ask God to forgive them for the sins that they have committed (or are still committing) as a result of the abuse that was forced upon them, as *no one* asks to be abused.

<u>The following simple prayer can be used as a guide</u>

Jehovah God, I am sorry for my sins of (**You Say What The Sin Is**). *Please cleanse me from* (**You Say What The Sin Is**). *I repent of and forsake* (**You Say What The Sin Is**). *Please help me to become you child and walk in your will. Thank you for your grace upon my life. Amen.*"

4. After they have confessed and forsaken their sins, that by the power of the Holy Spirit they would become blessed (empowered to prosper God's way);

5. They will learn how to live and walk in God's ways, which are not hard or grievous.

Although unorthodox in the literary community, I now direct these words of life to the author, Moses T(homas) Alexander Greene, II.

To the author, the son of my youth, I thank and praise God for giving me the opportunity to bring you forth. My children—Moses, Derek, Kaliah and Keith—are four of Heaven's Best. Next to knowing Jesus as Lord and Savior of my life, being your mother has been the greatest joy of my life. Parenting you has taught me faith, prayer, determination, persistence and to believe the promises of God. For He said that if I walked uprightly before Him, my children would be mighty in the land. As you and your siblings become mighty in the land, remember to always take the Lord along with you everywhere you go. He is a faithful God.

My son, "*bring for all the talents, skills and abilities that God has given you.*" Be not ashamed of the Gospel of Jesus Christ for it is the only power along with His blood that can truly save and heal a person. "*Moses, Bring Forth.*"

To my husband, Moses Thomas (Alexander) Greene, Sr., thank you for being "the best" father to your children that you knew how to be. Thank God for your presence in our lives.

Finally, to each reader, **TO BE GOD BE THE GLORY FOR ALL THE THINGS THAT HE HAS DONE AND WILL DO THROUGH "MY PROPOSAL: NOTHING BUT A GRACECHILD."**

Mrs. Betty Faye Brown-Greene
October 20, 2001
9:54 AM

the heart of
a prodigal desert baby

CHAPTER 1

*"Abandonment
is about understanding what my heart feels
and my mind codes as having occurred;
not what you intended. You understand?"*

-1 past 28
2:21 pm

RAW UNDERSTANDING
in theBuff of "It's Time To Take A Bath, Boys"

I have a non-blood family member.
She knows who she is.
She left me...when I was about ten.
My aunt left me.
I now understand life.
For years I was mad that she didn't give me so much as a good-
bye.
She didn't write us, she didn't write me.

When she came over, there was laughter in my house.
When she was there she would tell these exciting stories of going
to California and her working at either A&S or Alexander's I
can't remember which one.
She would...just be.

She brought
Balance into our house
          and on my vacation.
She was God's "peace be still"
To me.
She left.

I now understand life.

I
(and even at 26 I'm fighting back the tears of this reality)...
I was just an opportunity cost.
She made her flight.
Didn't
(Now I know)
Couldn't
Look back
And I was just an opportunity cost.

Not that she didn't love me,

Not that it wasn't hard for her to walk away from us,
From me...I mean y'all, she was allowed to give us baths.
No one else
Including family was allowed to do that...

But me,
   my being,
   my well-
   being
   wasn't enough to outweigh her need to go.

I understand.

   I *still* think life would have been different.

But I understand.

You don't ever need to contact me...
Really to utter one word of explanation...
Because I've lived a little bit now.
I know what it
Feels
Like that if
You

Just

Don't

Take

Flight
You will die...
Slowly...
With a cancer in your heart and mind.

Thank you

Thank you

Thank you.

man-sized understanding

The Lord shared with me when I turned
25 years old that He had some
Tremendous
Life-changing blessings
For me.
Age 25 into 26 is when I became a man.

I understand why
My dad comes in the house
And just goes up to his room.

Sometimes what you wanted to happen
       within yourself
       and
       within your home
Are so vastly
Different
Than the reality you come home to every night
That your only retreat is your
Bedroom.
It's not that you're not
       completely
       and
       wholly grateful
For the family you have

And its not that you

Don't realize how blessed you are,

It's that you need time

To get somewhere...

Somewhat familiar,

Where you can do inventory.

Where you look at your life,
       your choices,
       the direction of your life
       and that of those closest
       and furthest from you
       and you try to get it together to get it right.

Hey dad...
Right never comes.
Grace always shows up.
That has been one of the blessings of this year.
I've stopped trying to be perfect.
I've stopped trying to be so
Spiritually minded that I can't see the
       practical,
       natural,
       responsive side of Jesus Christ in the situations I find
myself in. M-
My house,

My apartment is

Full of people

And the immediate reaction when I enter

And see someone unexpectedly

Is that I have an attitude.

No one knows the

b r e a t h

Of relaxation

That I gave when I stepped out my car
And the need for
Replenishment that
I stand in need of.

That is what I'm panting after:

A chance to get home,
[and] be
with my God
before more demands of me to be more than what I am
without Christ are made.
It's not moody...
It's just not right.

But right never comes.

acceptance speech...rightly marginalized

I
God thank to like would
...have I friends the for

and I mean real friends.

I
year this learned
,friend a that

and I mean a real friend

not is
,there is who person the
...closest the is who

,friend a but

and I mean a real friend

one the is
.you for praying is who

LEFT: revelation for those

You know where you are

You know who is there...

You know who is closest...

You know where you are

You know who is not there...

You know who is furthest...

You know where you are

Find who is praying...

And there you will find your friend.

Just because you are in a far country doesn't mean that your heart doesn't desire love.

the most beautiful unanswered invitation

To this day, you remain the most beautiful specimen....

> *The first time you and I were introduced was two or three years ago. We spoke about the Pre-Grammy Gospel Party you attended hosted by Natalie Cole. Since that time I've wanted to tell you that you have a beautiful spirit. In case you didn't know, the encasement of your spirit is equally as stunning (smile). That Sunday afternoon you were more than just striking. This is it: if I was asked to bestow upon the totality of your being a name which would embody the essence of those few moments, it would be, "Simply Beautiful." You...all of you, Schyler, literally took my breath away.*

To this day you remain the most beautiful specimen...

> *First I noticed the way of your praise. You were standing up, clapping and praising GOD and something about your praise just caught my eye. When service was over Myron introduced us. Audibly, the reality, "She's beautiful," escaped from within, past my lips before I could even capture it. Since that Sunday, I have found myself at various times still intrigued by the indelible imprint your spirit and outer beauty have left on my mind and in part, in my heart.*

To this day you remain the most beautiful specimen...

> *If you would graciously allow, I would now like God, time and chance to grant me opportunity to get to know and experience the richness of who you are and desire to be. I desire to know Schyler. For one reason: Because*

...

To this very day, now <u>years</u> later, having been on television and movie sets, at network industry gatherings with literally hundreds of what this world defines as its "most beautiful" people and having visited Atlanta and now residing in Chocolate City, Washington, D.C

...

You Still Remain <u>The</u> <u>Most</u> <u>Beautiful</u> and <u>Breathtaking</u> Specimen of God's Awesome and Wonderful Female Creation That I Have Ever Seen.

invitation unanswered. just because you are in a far country doesn't mean that your heart doesn't desire love.

POTPOURRI

Chapter 1

I hate sitting at a table when every body knows (the same) nothing but acts like they all got it together.
Everything. Everything. Everything coming down.

Chapter 2

Never think you know every thing. It's the same day of your fall. The same day.
My daddy thought he knew, we thought we knew, and his rib, our sustenance, lived knowing she didn't know but maintained a thespiana existence for us.

Chapter 3

I could never be a woman. No matter how close I lived to and was nurtured by my mother's heart- I still never had her heart.
Not that in her staying she didn't try to give it to me but I don't now, nor did I ever have the heart of my mother. I extol You O Lord for creating me me as I never could have existed and endured the things a woman's heart must and did. NEVER

REVELATION

Thespiana. You name one woman who hasn't played this role and I'll show you a woman who never met a man. I'm not saying there is blame at the foot of the man; Primarily or Solely or Soully. It's just created in us. It is the how of how we communicate. It is the meta.

*From Sarah down to your present. Thespiana Sarah. Her stage: Going into a strange land where her man, <u>her</u> covering who is living out <u>his</u> promise, tells her, "Act like my sister...just for a little while, baby...because you're **too** beautiful."*
Mm. Picture that. Having to play the role because you're too what God made you. Too you for him. Not the real Him but just him. Say her name, "Patti! Patti!" Or the hers. Thespiana Patti is long gone. Sarah.

CONTINUALIE

What man enjoys playing the role of Thespiana? Not a one. Even the dressed up ones and the bottoms don't have the true heart of Thespiana. A true Thespiana can play the role and have the grace not to hurt through it. A thespian trying to be thespiana of any kind continually hurts. Continually. Continualie. Continual-lie.

In Genus species Bib-latin: *la Barrena thespiana*

Thespiana Sarai. Telling Abram, suggesting even, that, to appease the situation at hand—a word from God and no provision, less than none— "in true Thespiana form" the rib of the father of the faithful contorts and configures her mouth and her heart and the grace on her life to give power to the words—"Maybe you may want to sleep out tonight. M..m..May..be Hagar." Mm. I could **never** have the heart of Thespiana. I now believe the faith needed for a woman-child to survive the canal is to have the heart of Thespiana.

GRADUATION

I know. We were together for eternity. She was ahead of me. In line first.
She turned around. That's why she...she... There comes a moment in time, one, when you can't turn around. "HART NOOOOOOOOOO! HART NOOOOOOOOO!"

What's that sound? Where's that light coming from? Why R you pullin' on me? Get off!! I'm in line next. Noooooo! I'm going this way. The way of my Har...Noel tell him. Tell them, no! Noey!! I can't be a thespian. (why did I make an emphasis on the n) Nooo. She's suppos..sup...Huh? You savages. Get your hands off me. Get your hands off my body. Stop touching me!! Stop touching me! It's not supposed to take all of this to get to where I'm supposed to be...Nooo. She's suppo-, suh pose-. Noooooooooo!!

LEFT BACK

I'm cold. My HEART. Where is she? Where is she? NOOO!!!Eeee!!!YYYeLLLLL!!!!

Get that out my mouth! What are you putting up my nose!! Nooo!!

Where is she? I'm waiting. Where is she? I'm waiting? I'm cold. My H...

HEART-FELT KNOWLEDGE

I now know. I no longer just believe the faith needed for a sister-girl to survive the eerie canal is the heart of thespiana. Where do broken baby HEARTS go? I don't know...without mine I still have mine.

I Never Knew I Needed To Be Washed:
no prose, no poetry, just my reality

I Never Knew I Needed To Be Washed...until then.

For years I had helped <u>them</u> sing,
"*Amazing Grace...that saved a wretch like me*,"
Never believing that I was what
*They*were singing
      and repeating themselves to be.
And then the lie would continue,
"*I once was lost, but now am found.*
 Twas blind but now I see."

I accepted Christ into my heart
At age seven.
And I knew what I was doing.
And the Holy Spirit came upon me
At seven when I was getting baptized.
Uncontrollable tears.
Not emotion, true praise.
When was I lost? When was *I* blind?
You wouldn't
Believe how I know,
But I have always had a consciousness of God.
Always.

In Grandma's basement when Della let me play her record player,
I would play "aREAthaFRANKkins" classic Gospel album.
(The one where she is sit'in' down.
    I think she shows her bare feet and has that thing on-
    majestically wrapped around her head
    like my mom does when she's rushing to get to the
market Saturday mornings). And I would shout....
For real.

Years later I looked back and
Knew then that it was real.
That alone,
Without
A cowd,
Alone I had God.

I never knew *I* needed to be washed.
Not by works of righteousness which I have done – but
According to the Family, It always treated
All Its kids based on their works of righteousness.
Who got the solos? The good kids. Who got to do offering?
The good kids. Who got to give the guest pastor a token of our
appreciation?
The good kids.

I was always glad to be in the service
One mo' time.
In fact, I was
So glad that I never stayed home. Even at age 11,
            7:45 service,
            Sunday School,
            main service, and
            afternoon service,
                    (at my church and *especially* away),
was my ritual. And even if I was home,
Most of the time I was in service.
And on the soccer fields,
Instead of playing my position I was in service.
And in first or second grade,
            or maybe it was kindergarten,
My teacher had to call my mother and
Ask her to tell me to stop having revival service
            and baptism service
on the playground to the right of the swings during recess.
And when I would go shopping with mom,

dad and
Derek,
I would always be singing.
So when was I
in need of a bath?
When?
My heart was pure...(towards God).

I don't know why Jesus loves me,
I don't know why he cares,
I don't know why he sacrificed his life,
oh, but I'm glad, so glad he did.

Lie for verse 1,
Lie for verse 2,
And lie for verse 3a.
And everybody know I am glad.
(Like "everybody know grandma's sugah bad.")

But I did.
I knew
Why Jesus loved me. I was loveable.
I did the right things.
I knew why he cared; because I cared for him.
Because I talked to him.
And I knew why he sacrificed his life:
He had to...
            to save me...
But I was just included in the package.
And how I was glad.
And how I was, "so glad" he did.

So that's why I would run the water,
            sit on the toilet and
            read or
            sing.

I would hear my Dad's bed creek from behind the pipes
And then from my seat, I'd thrash the water about in the tub
With my hands, making enough suds,
Because I knew why.
And I didn't *need* a bath.
One may have been desired by my Parents
But I didn't need to bather.

Tramaine and
Walter were my buddies.
And that was back when she was listed as "Tru-"
Ya know, they were *that kind of friends.*
James spoke
Peace and
Told me that *I was going through* and
Taught me early to ask God to *keep me in His care.*
Saturday mornings, my second favorite friend
Dorothy
Would come by faithfully at about 8:45 and
Coate me in an outfit of love.
She would tell me,
"*If you dig one ditch you better dig two.*
The trap you set may just be for you."
I never knew what she meant but
I wasn't supposed to...
She was...
Because she was older than me.
And my favorite friend,
Shirley,
The first time we met she called me up out of the audience one
night,
(When I was shorter than she was),
And rubbed my head or
My shoulders as she told a story.
Shirley was always telling stories.
And she *never* got in trouble for the stuff she made up.

In fact, folk would get to dancing
And shouted because of them.

So I was always around
Washed people.
Celebrated people.
I was always
Listening to music by washed people. Most of the times anyway.
So why do
I
have to wash up?
I want to be around these people all the time.
Not because it's
"The industry"
But because that's where the washed meet
And do binnness.
I have the passion for stardom and
For traveling and
Love You, like they do.
You know I won't fall. I am one of the washed,
Like them,
And none of them are dirty.
Being dirty is not even in any of their songs.
They just sing about being clean and
Serving the *big* Mr. Clean.

I won't get dirty.
On purpose or
Off purpose or
Roundabout purpose—I just won't
Ever get dirty.
I wouldn't do that to You.
I love You.
I don't even want to have sex
Until I'm married. That's clean.

And the full impact of being molested won't come out for years to
come.
I'm not taking a bath. Others need one, I don't.
My heart is right.
The pee-pee kid Boom-Boom needs one, I don't.
You can look at him AND
smell him a mile away.
None of my washed friends stink and
I see them every Saturday.
I don't need a bath.
 I don't need
To wash up and honestly
Will never need to wash.

"Mo-Mo, it's time to take a bath!"
"Mommy no!" my heart exclaims.
"moMO!"
That's Daddy. "Dad, can you wait till "Gimme A Break" goes off!"
It's Saturday night.
I wish he'd stop calling my name.
I did a good wash-up this morning. Come on, I don't need a full
bath tonight.

I
've been
               too good
               to bathe.
I
'm not taking a bath.
Tell my brother to bathe
               "cause I
                       don't
                       need
                       one."
He needs one and
You know it.

If I had as much as
You had given him,
I
'd be washing up
and bathing everyday.
I
'd be the cleanest cat You made. But
he got   records
            and
            records
            and
            all these gifts
            and
            still is dirty.
If it were *me*, as soon as
I
'd slide in the mud,
            in any mud,
I
'd wash it off.
Especially if it was
            the same mud.
"Buh he doan warsh."

You can look   at the people around him
            and   at his friends
            and   tell that he ain't
hardly thinkin' about washin'.
You ain't given me what you gave him
            and even if You did,
            especially if You did,
I wouldn't be
Staying in the hogpen   ...
                just lying there   ...
                prostrate
                in a prodigal state...

Mirrors, garbage and swine all around me....
Every thing
      and
Every pore soiled with mucky dark-brown,
                  cherry-brown,
                  light-brown,
                  beige
      and   cream
                  churned up,
                  quick-sandular mire.
I'
ve been
too good to take a bath
and
I
Just
Ain't
Takin'
1!

From the 12th verb of the 18th Pro.
Go back to Sesame Street: "P"..."RIDE"... "PRIDE." Letterman,
start the countdown.

10
<u>After a Bethphage Rehearsal</u>
"How come you don't
Hug me like you
Hugged that light-skinned boy?"

A huh?-thought.

NINE <u>Phone confab about the Rehearsal</u>
"Who's the
Light skinned boy?"
 "You are, dummy."

"Me. I'm not
Light-skinned."
"You are."
"Anyway, so what's the point? He was mad that
Jon Daniel was giving me a hug?"

"Moses, Liam is gay."
A huh?-thought

8
<u>To my college pastor</u>
"I just don't understand how one could be so anointed-"
Wisdom tried to shut my mouth, cut me off,
But I ignored her.

SEVEN <u>from my First Lady</u>
"Moses, that's just a spirit that when it gets a
Hold of a man,
It's very strong and
It's very hard to get it ou—"
-Dismissed in my mind that she
Couldn't fully understand
What I was saying.
I was talking about people of the cloth,
Not the washcloth.

6
<u>Back to the pastor</u>
"But he's married."
"And what is that supposed to mean?"
A *BIG*-Huh-thought.

FIVE <u>of the Bethphage Choir</u>
"...And Moses that's why I had to stop singing in that choir."

"Huh?"
"That choir is known for it."
"It is?"

4
<u>In Grad School</u>
"Oooo, Moses, I heard that a trustee from your church was caught~"

~I block them out.
I got to get to him for myself. Ask my own question.
I get to him, to his office.

"What's the problem?"
"Brother, they're talking about you."
"And? Moses, Disney is over; you need to grow up."
"HUH?"
"Moses, Disney is over; you need to grow up."

What are you saying?!
I need a denial
Spoken
By your lips.
Tell me it's a lie.
Just say it.

THREE <u>**At the Bethphage Choir's Anniversary**</u>
"Is that a blouse that man has on?"
"Huh?"
"Amana that's a blouse!"
"Ohhhh, my God!" she says
Cracking up uncontrollably. "Oh my God,
That's prettier than any blouse I even own!"
"Is that lace?"

I don't understand yet.
I'm washed, they're
Singing about a washed life.
I...I...I don't *want* to understand this.
"Are those finger waves and rhinestones?!#"
Now I join in Amana's laughter.

2
<u>To my recently restored friend</u>
"I just don't see how you could be
So anointed
          and have
Such a powerful ministry
          and
          can't
          shake
          that
          thing!
I mean here I am...asking,
Pleading with God
For an anointing like this and
This guy has one but won't shake this spirit.
I just don't
Understand.
You know what I'm saying?
It
Would
Not
Be
Me!"

I
I never knew I needed to be washed until I fell...
and
I
couldn't

get
up.

I never knew I needed to be washed until I was already down...
And I fell inconceivably- to my mind, to my flesh's confidence-
Deeper.

I couldn't get up.
On the other side of the wall the prophet faced me and sang,
"Gotta get on up."
I couldn't.
I could get
It up, but
I
Couldn't get up.
In fact,
It
Never stayed down.
It was like sensory pathways I never had before awakened
Loooooong past adolescence.

I never thought I needed to be washed.
My thought was my reality but to get the connection,
          to live in an awareness,
God had to allow me to be brought
Past my thought-life
          into knowledge.
Knowledge is always experience.
Shouldn't be, but it is.
I never knew I needed to be washed until I
Knew that I had fallen.
Until I knew,
          "wait,
          this experience goes past my perception of me in the
          Body. I am experiencing mind-altering knowledge days
          that are so much deeper than feelings."

The Family never treated me like I did
Or would ever need to be washed.
What then, no,
How then do I make sense of this experience?
You don't; you live it out.
I'm trying to diagnose the problem
As I'm straddling.
No double mind,
No Heckell-Jyde mind can prescribe any remedy.
What then, yes,
How then is
This experience in
This far country going to bring God glory?

Mm.
Because
            you're
                dealing with it.
You have told folk, and heaven
And earth have heard,
"I know I need to be washed."
That which you
Gloried in has become of
None effect.
That for which you were praised
            in Jerusalem
Has been stripped
            in Babylon.
You gloried in a deliverance that
Wasn't your own like you were
Of your own.
And that which
The Father
            suffered
            you

> not
> > to have gone through
> > back home
> Is become familiar
> > as home
> > in exile;
> That God might prove your heart and
> Humble your being to a
> > grace understanding alone.
> It's not the series of acts and actions...He's
> Proving your heart. He's
> Proving that which desires to be
> > ruddy,
> > countenance-beautiful and
> > goodly to look to.

You don't come into worship with your hands lifted and your heart on the Family's pedestal, [why?]...you know you need to be washed. You don't even want to lift your hands; because you know that this week they have been washed. You can't even follow your Jerusalem routine – 9 o'clock Sunday School, 11 o'clock service—you have to sneak into the 6:30 service, smnh, the "Deliverance service." Not because you're working so long and late but because Sunday mornings have now become your weekly battle time and

the battle lasts all day.

Waking up ready for God's glory. Struggling not to make that call. Fighting against the speed limitless law of The Flesh (in Lust County, WS—that is Whatever State your mind is in). Warring in your mind not to replay moment by moemeant the what, when, where, why and hows of your mind's ponderings of the last time it almost did or did not happen. The last time you got close but Christ rose mighty; toiling not to calculate when did the four de play begin in your skull; when did the taste, the sensation, the feen or Phine in your blood recognize, "it's time for another hit." Walking fast and talking faster, (to only yourself); mouthing without the power of voice "I'm not going there," "I'm taking another way to church...I'm not even going in that direction" or "It's not going to happen this morning." No. This Sunday morning you absolutely, without denial and actually, a little bit of being in denial, win the battle. Jah, Ha   Le   Lu!

Then

veryrushedandsuddenlyitseemslikeGODHimselfwantstoseeyoufall becauseyoumadeitoutaliveinthespiritofyourmind.You

go

t
h
e

o
t
h
e
r

d
i
r
e
c
t
i
o
n
,

you

don't

take that hit,

you

don't make that call,

you **don't**

dropbythe

        apartment
or
            condo
or
              house
or
                shack
or
                    mobile home
or
                      mansion

and you are feeling, (not even knowledge yet, you are just "feeling"), the VICTORY over   sin,
satan
and self.

You are about to leave your apartment to go the right direction only to fin-

"R
    r
        r
            r
                r
                    r
                        r
                            r
                                i
                                    n
                                        g."

Or
"Bzzzzzzzzzzzzzzzzzzzzzzzzzzzzzzzzzzzzzzzzzzzzzzzzzz."

The phone, the cellular rings. The pager's vibrations take a Northeastern Direct, non-stop, Metro-linering express ride from your hip's side to the place of panic in your heart. You don't even want to **LOOK**down at it
                    BUTyou decide
                    TOlook down,
to go to the caller i.d. But you get victory...again.
You leave,
Seeing the temptation
And head for service.

But
Ahhhhh,
As you drive or
As you walk to the train you remember you   ignored
                that...
                that HIM
Who told you to do this last night, but now you have to make one stop—
At the gas station for some mints or to get gas or to Mickey Dees for change for the offerings because you didn't get any the night b-b-bbbe........ fore........ and......

YOURheart
ISsome
WHEREbe
TWEENa
RACEand a p-p-p-puh-puh-puht-t-t-t-ttter
because

hhhhHHh-he,
sh-sh-shhhhHHh-he,
it,

your thorn,
your weakness is
there at the gas station.
They're on their way to their own service but he or she has to use
the bathroom
And your house is right around the corner
Or on the way,
Or they got a bloody nose
Or locked keys in their car
Or missed the bus and will miss the same service you're going to,
Or got a flat, sumthin'.

Some **"thing"** has happened such that she or he, your it, your
thorn, your
weakness is in your   face

with
a need.

I've never been one for games, Lord. It took a total spillage of
bleach in my mind combined with drinking three mugs of hyssop
tea and a mixture of hyssop paste applied to my chest with a
hyssop brush (like Vick's vapor rub on my 7-year old congested
chest) for me not to answer the call, and I've set my flesh into a

jail (at least until service is over) and with all of that You allow this?

That's the "introspective, reserved me" that speaks while still in denialbutIamcomingoutofmyimmediatedenialand I am in SHOCK!

LORD,

what

r

U

doing!

I'm *trying* to get to church!

So you find out theneed and you don't want to be the one who is there; you want to do the Christian thing but now in yourHeckellJyde mind you have become Lot's oldest gal: you only see one way out. You don't call for help, you can't call for prayer. E'erbody (pronounced like those from Babylon) is in Church. So then, partly disappointed with God, you resisting you handle the surprise in full you.

I never knew
I needed to be washed until even in a situation like this,
Who am I kidding, in
Situationshuns
Like these,
I found that there was still a place
      in my mind,
        in my own inwards yearning
To touch some thing,
        some nook,
        some cranny of flesh, some how...
Even
On my way to my Father's house—
Even while already dressed up
On my way to my Father's House
           on His day.
Even with the emergency handled
And the way of escape a step away,
The doors I had prayed locked
("keep my mouth set on Sight-acceptable meditations") ,

The on-duty security guard and
The full-time jockey assigned to secure
                        and bridle my tongue
Would fight against the stirrings of bee-entrenched sweetness
In the dead pathways of my heart for this person
       or particular experience
       or specific rush
And somehow lose.

The doors would swing open,
       the security guard would go on rounds
            and
       the jockey desired a French-inspired tumble.
All three of them would concede victory to the living death within
my members and allow my mouth to declare,
"Good seeing you, again.
Can I have a hug?"
       or
"Now that I know you're all right,
I'm gonna
       still
       make my way to church.
Is my tie all right?"
(Knowing a touch was all it took for a
       moemeant of
       instant,
       quik-made hell
       to ignite).

By 6:30 I had it together, to at least get to the House.
Carried only by grace.
I
Might have been dazed while I
       was there,
       intoxicated by the reality of
       my own heart's power to reign supreme

in Jehovahliness in one moment
But then
pursue mercilessly
after markmissing the next,
But (Hallelujah)
I
was
in
the House.
I had been taught enough in Jerusalem by my mama to know to
"<u>get</u>
to
the House."

The fact that I made it there—
driving or
for a season
of seasons bussed,
bmw'd
(black man walking),
metroed,
tom+
jerried
and/
or   cabbed—
Was my "Hallelujah",
Was my holy hands lifted,
my "dance, dance, dance, dance, dance, dance, dance all
night,"
my "-all the time"
and
my "God is good-" call and response.

Communion Sundays.
Berkeleyized melodies with McKayed lyrics became my truths.

I'm still here.
I'm still here.
I made it through, so have you.
I've been through the fire and I've been through the flood,
I'm still here, kept by his Love.

Dirty, I
      couldn't
            praise.
Fellowship
      had
      been
            broken.
The enemy was *reminding* me not accusing me;
      and
      not of what was
Thought to have
"Might-*of*-happened" the Monday before,
      but
Of what
I
      did
Moemeants,
            sometimes
Many,
Mini
Moemeants earlier that afternoon.

I
couldn't   couldn't
repeat   repeat
repeat what pastor was telling us to tell our neighbors
      because
I
      didn't

feel worthy.
Before now,
        before this season
        of seasons,
        some aspect
        of me
Always felt worthy.
He never died for a sinner like me,
        but like you.
I,
          with my good self,
        was just included in the number.

Have you ever known you were washed,
White as snow,
But felt dirty?
Smelled dirty?
Had dirty veins?
Filthy pores?
Fowl breath?
Fowl breath
With a fowler's heart?
I hadn't...not before...but now,
I
am the first plunged one into the
Fountain from God with us' veins.
I now
understand
why my culture repeats chorus
        after chorus
        after chorus of its hymns
        and its songs.
Each chorus plows deeper into the brokenness,
            past the rocks of accusation,
            past the pebbles of camouflage
        and

into the devil-colored earthworm
dung mounds of your reality
to a place of undeserved,
pre-you crucified knowledge:

"<u>You   Are   Washed</u>."

That's a whole lot of choruses, let me tell you.

I never knew
I needed to be washed until
I looked back
And remembered that sin
Is not
Only what you do
But also
That on which you meditate.
Contemplate.

EPIPHANY.

"Oh."

Then,
I began to see God's Sovereignty in my life,
on my mind,
on my meditations and
non-actions.

Now, not only do I sing,
"Through meh-KNEE-ee-ee DAY-ayyy-ay-ay 'Njers twaohils and
snares.
  Ah have all reh-DÆ- E come"
        like Phoebe Dowdell,
(I always sang that line because I
Grew up with spiritual warfare against asthma),
        but

I also have learned to crawl...to go back to verse 1.
I am included amongst those of 1.
I am included in the number who sing,
"Amazing grace how sweet the sound,
That saved a wretch like me..."

I was a wretch suffered by the hand of God not to be wretched. I
was wretched in the spirit of my mind. I once (and not now that I
know I have fallen and had fallen many times before)-   Read.
        Listen.
        Hear.
        Understand.
        Apply.

You cannot and
I cannot
        reduce my "once" to "an experience."
If it stops at the experience
there is no healing.
If I stop at the experience
there is no access to the Father.

My once is a place of knowledge.
The purpose of the experience was to (Hallelujah) bring me to a
knowledge base- that it is from the beginning,
        with my lack-of-solos-
        lack-of-doing-offering self,
        from my earliest recollections of self,
        in my days of playing Areatha Franklin's albums
        in Grandma Doll's basement,
        during my solo concerts on the ceramic tile floor
        in the basement before an always sold-out crowd
        of exposed pipes in the ceiling, and
        in my tears in the baptismal pool,
Back then
        and

Before then is when   was lost.

Therefore, it is with knowledge
          (which you must have to get wisdom which leads to
understanding)
that I now sing,
"I'
ahhhhhhhh onnnnnnccccccce wuh-uh-uhz lost but NOW, bu-uh-
uh-uh-uh-t now, right now
I'
m found 'twuhz blind but now I see."

<u>ONE</u>
"Lord, I now know that I always needed to be washed and still yet
need to be washed."

Silence.

One of the axioms of communication is that silence connotes affirmation.

Mm, what an "amen" God must then be giving Himself for the words I just expressed out of the many, mini shatterings of my heart's brokenness and my spirit's introduction to true ruefulness.

The silence concerns me.

JUDGMENT?

mercy?

What, Lord? Just say something?

Lord, PLEASE!

"NOW I DON'T NEED A SUPERSTAR..."

Tears fall.

From both of us.

HIS anoint my head to do greater work; mine, the ground to receive it.

" 'CAUSE I'VE ALWAYS ACCEPTED YOU AS YOU ARE; [CAUSE I DECLARED YOUR SHALL BE WAY BACK THEN], YOU WON'T BE DENIED BECAUSE I AM NOW SATISFIED WITH THE HUMILITY THROUGH WHICH YOUR HEART HAS CRIED."

The words He has chosen to sing unto me p i e r c e through
the silence, directly to me...in my right now—a hellish segue before
my exaltation which simultaneously reduces and strengthens me
to the first true exhale of my life. Before I cast myself into the
limelight of an abyss of apologies, woes and thank-yous within, the
Master says,

*"NOW, THAT YOU KNOW YOU ALWAYS NEEDED WASHED,
BUILD."*

Silence, but not as a sign of immediate affirmation from me, so I guess to pot with that self-evident truth. My heart, mind and soul are trying to piece it together.

He knows I have a question about that last word, that last five-letter directive that He just gave. I respond as one who has set at the pool, (called BETHESDA in the Hebrew), for years waiting for help,

"But God, there... there...there's no glory here. Just mess and the most pain, the most sorrow I've ever felt in my life. There's been confusion and babelli-"

"-NOW, THAT YOU KNOW," the Master Interrupts, *"BUILD."*

Now that I know...build. A big Huh-thought.

"I don't know why Jesus loves me, I don't know why He cares,
I don't know why He's told me to build **now**,
oh...but for the mere fact that He *still* wants to use me,
oh but I'm glad, so glad He did."

I never KNEW I needed to be washed. I don't profess to know much, but I know, even today, I yet need to be washed. This is what I will tell on the mountains to which I am sent. No prose, no poetry, just an exiled experience with the Master.

Now that *you* know, build.

exiled to BABELLON

CHAPTER 2

There are some things
-that although only seeds-
were sown into you...

> *about you...*
> *before you ...*
> *and in time, ...*
> *out from you...*

which,
at an inevitable time of reaping,
make you the perfect candidate
for a settlement to an exile land.

If you don't understand God,
past His acts to His ways,

> *(and I didn't)*

you will wrestle against
and give credit to the enemy
without knowing it is the hand of God
vaccinating you past rumors
to a refined reality.

> *The exile*
> *is the first step to a new you.*

Backstory: 1:29 AM   Can't wait for my call to come stand before the Board and get the date that I get released. I want to tell Maurice, face-to-face, that with all he's been through I learned the lesson. Even being locked up with hosts of my brothers and even a couple of sisters, I learned the lesson. Some lessons just need to be learned before parole. Maurice would agree.

Episode #67654
The "Attempted" Circumcision of
Maurice, Thornet, Leroy , Lee and me

The Problem: He sent the help, but the help had the same exact problems that those on trials had, but those on trials were made the scapegoat; a convenient camouflage for rampant, lusting hearts in the Church.

They missed it...and are missing it. According to the Word, sexual perversion is *any* sexual act that occurs outside the spiritual covenant of marriage, heterosexual relations included. Fornication, the parallelogram to sexual perversion, is any sexual act that occurs outside the spiritual covenant of marriage, including same sex relations.

Hmnh. Everybody knows that Deris, the tenor saxophonist and bass player of the church is out there having sex outside of marriage, (heterosexual sex but sex nonetheless), but that's not on trial. The music director of the Turnicheke Mass Choir, fine Sister Justyne Russell, she too calls her inner circle people and tells Michael, a platonic, brother-like friend from yesteryear, that he cannot come over because her man may drop in. Sex in the city, oh, but she's not on trial. The guy who sat behind you in service yesterday, David, he has pornography pictures in a safe place on his laptop, but he's not on trial. He's a trustee and the chair of the security ministry. He wears more make-up than Tammy Faye...but you're looking in the wrong place with the wrong eyes; that's why you've yet to see it.

The Place: The town was transformed into a kind of Biblical city of refuge because God commanded circumcision for flesh-hearted, sexual iniquity. I mean, how else can you explain three fellas from Jerusalem just ending up in Babylon with one of their exiled brothers they all knew growing up except it be the hand of God re-positioning his -jireh to meet their heart's needs for the men they will be seasons from now. It wasn't about the mess pre-supposedly going on. It was about someone being able to say, "me too."

The Story: Four guys, all with struggles of some kind of sexual perversion, were in town for spiritual surgery.

The Characters:

Maurice Aman Jones

Fact: In town to go through circumcision for masturbation, pornography, complete deliverance from the propensity for homosexual acts before, during and after marriage, heterosexual adultery, over-accommodations of the heart, and inordinate affection. **Truth:** What got Mau exiled here was that he began to articulate to GOD a willingness to understand the gaps in his life and of his desire for mighty usage by Him. By this reason, he fulfilled his ministry purpose in Jerusalem. However, so that he wouldn't look to return to Jerusalem or heed to the false prophets bi-weekly speaking, "God is calling you back home," Jehovah allowed a whirlwind of *babbling* amongst those Mau had spiritually fed all his life to take place. The final stirring of caffeine to his Properly, prodigally-placed steps was a wound by home for nothing more than having a simple heart that didn't understand life or the ways of real life. He left Jerusalem injured and arrived in Babylon in search of healing from his sexually abused past and religiously misunderstood present.

Thornet Cleveland Proctor

Cousin of Maurice's best friend back home, Martin. Canonized (somewhat "evangelized") as "the most beautiful, unloved man you will ever meet."

Fact: A thirty-something professional Tommy sleeping on Maurice's Thomasville. (We think he's a software engineer or webmaster, but no one knows for sure). Surgery Procedure:

I.   Radical Circumcision for Sex and Lust

      a.   Through   Heterosexual   (and   Possibly Homosexual) sex acts

          i.   Pornography

              1.   Live

                  a.   Watching

                  b.   Possibly being watched

              2.   Video

                  a.   Watching

                  b.   Possibly being watched

Truth: Living the consequences of one wrong moment in time. Who doesn't? *He is past wounded.* There are (seemingly) no balms in Gilead, Jerusalem, Babylon or anywhere he takes flight. His flight, instability, and the very ordering of his steps are all in search for the balm. We, the Church, treat Thor like *We are the* first to be smacked with the knowledge that he needs surgery. Although it's *his* heart and *his* heart's flesh that has hardened, We are the ones who constantly speak, "He's too old to still be-" without knowing the whys of him ending up in Babylon...and back to Jerusalem...and onto Corinth...and laid over in Ephesus and stationed in Ammon and...

Leroy Hunter Petersen

Maurice and Thor's first roommate.

Lived two Sunday School bus stops from Mau's house growing up. **Fact:** Circumcision for pornography and a heart for stuff he chooses not to even acknowledge (as evidenced by lingering eyes and his three-too-many "good-going-pats" on the court and in the locker room of his heart's unspoken desire). **Truth:** Almost thirty and still trying to measure up to that unspoken male approval: the head-nod up in the hallways of the high school called Life. He is the wounded breath of the party, which is, even on the best of days, still halitosis. As purposeful in natural living as a compass that has fallen from a skyscraper and gingerly slammed against slabs of raw, unfinished marble, God has given him high-falutin', blue vein societal privilege to counter his blemished familial existence. If we opened our eyes long enough to record an observation, he only wants male validation: the earthly, however non-existent, male shaddai to speak "man enough."

Liam Gao Chanshik Osemwegie (Lee)

Fact: The product of a Nigerian's missionary trip to mainland China, he and Mau have been friends since their families met one August evening by the bathrooms at Six Flags in Nazareth back in '79. He is a journey.

A recent graduate from Mau's alma mater, he was picked up by the Babylonian Stallions, a development team. Heaven's reality is that he's here to go through circumcision for lying, inordinate affection, soliciting prostitution, sex through homosexual behaviors and acts, sex through heterosexually - perverse behaviors and acts, and harloting his heart for any thing that will ordain him love or attention. **Truth:** The athlete's athlete, the exoticism of how God fashioned him—six-feet, three-and-one-quarter inches tall, a complexion legally intoxicated with sassafras tea, and a frame that distributes (with utmost excellence) the treasures of Africa Major and Asia Minor—immediately causes women *and men* to pause. When you see him from afar, Scripture comes alive; man *is* fearfully and wonderfully made! But up close, the hazel of his eastern-influenced eyes is not beauty, but loss. If We stuck around long enough to listen, hear, and pray, We would have received understanding that what he does, no, used to do, was in direct proportion to his search to get gain...from somewhere. The revolution in the colors of his eyes echoes the voids of his heart. He is, at 28, *still trying* to handle the pain; *still panting* to reclaim the brown; *still pursuing* every lead to the antidote for losing the one, central, male authority figure that defended, defined and named him; (and then being sanctified to nothing or no one). Lee lives bruised and wounded and thus wounds and leaves others with abrasions.

The Plan: There is a balm in Gilead for all the men but they have to deal with their Ammonites and Moabites to get to it. The scheduled operations were meant to make the four wounded men deal and heal. Instead, four mirrors in different stages all looked at one another saying, "Man, that reflection sure got some issues!" They all missed it. The four of them, as grown men, lived in the same city, (as grown men), and not once did they all gather together to intercede for their lusts and our iniquities. Not one time did these men or We, the Church, ever gather together collectively and bring the other's sexual addictions to GOD.

Maurice's life was on trial this past year. But while everyone of the House was watching Mau for his every action and reaction God was watching our hearts for their actions and reactions. We, the Church, pastors up to ushers, stood on the sidelines, made our observations, posted our bets and then participated with Maurice, Thornet, Leroy and Lee in the blame game. We all wormed our ways out of dealing with the truths of our own hearts, with each other and with the One. They missed it. We missed it. (Although it's not even my time I will include myself in that we.)

Wisdom's Lesson: This is the lesson: what puts your life on trial before the cameras come, (post-exilic but pre-exultation), is NOT the preponderance of sin. No, no, nooooo! You can look at the lives of Music Director of the Kisissimi M.A.S.S., I mean Turnicheke Mass Choir, Justyne, and also Trevor and Antoinette, the Directors of the Singles Ministry, to see that.

Parenthetical Selah Thoughts
Grace-Induced Delay of Trial: They've yet to be given a court appearance. Grace alone doesn't allow Maurice to wait with great joy for their trial dates. Grace alone, I tell you. It alone is grace that has tempered his heart to fall to its knees and enter the

intercession place. Their trials won't even come to the surface because he's recovering from the surgery.

Post-Op Recovery Instructions: The Good Doctor says, "Maurice, to keep swelling down and so that the staples are kept as clean as possible (until they come out), you need to stand in the gap and make up the hedge." It's a mighty hard task to have had a surgical procedure last longer than it was supposed to, in part, because everything familiar and some relationships you thought were familial, were making bets and taking picks on the outcome; and on top of that, you are Told that another's trial date won't even have to come to pass if you stay on your heart's knees. What kind of circumcision recovery instruction is that!

Wisdom's Lesson Continued: What puts your life on trial is one moment of public misjudgment. **Clarification:** Not "public misjudgment" but "misjudgment in public." **Wisdom's Lesson Continued...Again:** Maurice's heart was pure, long pure and pure long before he fell and the Church had already issued a Proclamation of Indictment. Not because things *were* going on, but because his *misjudgment in public* left the door wide open for speculation. **Clarification II:** Maurice told me yesterday, (he communes with me daily but Mondays are my day to receive wisdom from him), "I guess misjudgment in private, in the quiet places in your heart and in the privacy of your home is not misjudgment. It's what they call discretion." Hmnh.

Application Deathline: Because I'm so close to Maurice, I'll never miss it. I have watched the ministries of millions of my brothers unexpectedly and like a surge of overwhelming, Divine-reordering die just because they didn't understand discretion. Because I'm still so close to Maurice, I'll never miss it.

My Story, My Song: I Made A Vow Some Vows To The Lord:

1. I promise you God I won't miss it.

2. I will use Your power in me to shorten all of my brothers' trials by praying up Hosea-like hedges.

3. When I hear echoes of what my friends and even my enemies are going through reverberating against my own true heart's desires or, the times when I behold yeast-infective leaven in another's life—so distinctively familiar because I know what has come up against my own—I promise You that I will not use my tongue to choose my own hand-picked jury, (from a selection of my peers), to keep the court in recess...in a perpetual waiting for a verdict that only You can give.

    a. I'll declare a "change of venue," from earth to You such that Your virtues and Your mercy are reigned down into the second heaven for Michael, Gabriel and every effervescing, priestly spirit from the Throne to participate with the Archs for my brothers' lives.

4. I will speak to

    a. every man who, like Lazarus, has been long past dead, who has long past given up;

    b. every Mephibosheth who should be further but some one, some thing, some incident, some interruption happened and left him full of Godly intent but without an inward wherewithal to get to the table; LAME;

c.   every dry bone in the midst of his plush and greene valley that is in need of a resurrection life-powerful word to move him into Your predestinated pathway for his life.

And I will declare to You and You only his need for your mercy, considering myself lest I be tempted. Father, from one shepherd to Another, I purpose to have a tongue of mercy and intercession for those closest to me and seemingly furthest from You as I now have watched and observed and studied and know and understand that if it had not been for the Lord who was on Maurice's side, and if it had not been for you who was on my side, where would he or I (one-day) be?

FADE TO REAL-LIFE.

COMMERCIAL 1
COMMERCIAL 2
Station I.D.
Fade up:

Teasers for Episode #67655

A.   Act IV, Scene 3B

"This is a lesson for a man."

B.   Act I Scene 2C

"This is a lesson strictly for all men."

C.   Act IV Scene 2A

"This is not a lesson strictly for a minister...can't restrain this just to the Gospel."

D.   Act VII, Scene 4A

"My father is a man."

E.   Act I, Scene 1C

"This "attempted" circumcision of Maurice, Thornet, Leroy and Lee is not a lesson strictly for a minister...can't restrain this just to the Gospel."

Closing Credits—Scroll Down

"The understanding that came from Episode #67654 is dedicated to four outstanding and mighty men of God who hung close to Mau and stood as and by him during his surgery and subsequent trials."

Benedict Early

My boy Mo'Better:

What's up, man? You've been on my mind and I decided to write to throw some balance to your present trial-scope. Two words, one phrase: "Benedict early."

First, start rejoicing and I mean greatly rejoice. I heard that you've been going through some things. Listen, although now for a season it seems like God has determined that there is purpose for your daily heaviness through allowing a myriad of challenges and temptations to come up, in and against your life, rejoice. Mo, out of how I've seen God move in my own life, you're going through this because your faith is on trial. Court *is* in session. I know you're the one in court but whatever the charges, know this: it's not about you; it's about the quality and durability of your faith, little brother.

Mo, although you're heavy with a lot of things right now, this trying of your faith is so that your faith might be found to give God praise, honor and glory at the appearing of Jesus through your posture and attitude in your trial. Mo, think. It's that "p implies q" stuff we learned in freshman year Logic, (in which you got an "A" if I remember correctly—smile).

P: Gold is tried, proven and tested with fire before it comes forth in the pure purpose for which God designed it.

Q: Your faith is much more precious to God than gold that perishes.

Therefore, if gold has to be tried, proven and tested with fire before it comes forth in the purpose for which God designed it and your faith is much more precious to God than gold, then it is logical to assume (but for us as Christians something for us to know) that your faith will, at some point, be tried, proven and tested with fire before it comes forth in the pure purpose for which God designed it. And on top of that, it won't perish! I think I'm gonna shout in this jail cell by myself!! Mo, six-and-a-half words, two phrases: "Benedict early: [cuz] "It's just a purge." Why are you looking at this fiery trial as if it is a strange occurrence? Benedict early.

And I got a new phrase for you. "Be Sober. Be Vigilant". Man, I know you don't drink but people have been telling me they've seen you drunk, tipsy or under some thing's or some body's influence. They said, "Mo' Better's intoxicated with modeling and new opportunities and what Babylon can provide for him, and with people, his new church, and friendships." (**And,** I heard that there's possibly some straight-up, hot, butterball naked sex and fornication going on too.) Bruh? Bruh! You've got to be sober, man!

Seriously, Mo. Be sober. When it comes to the place of your heart and its real and perceived voids, and when it comes to your dreams and the timetable for these things to be accomplished, <u>don't</u> <u>lose</u> <u>your</u> <u>sobriety</u>. And I want you to be on the watch. Stop letting things take you by surprise. You gotta think like a vigilante. Seriously man, I want you to be cunning and wise in and with your vigilance but be vigilant nonetheless. You're not walking around in Disney World or in some Wonderland environment. This is life.

I'm not getting on you. Trust, I've been there and I know about those times when, in your heart, you really want to do good but what ends up happening is that you do the opposite. Brother, been there. But I've gotta stress these points of sobriety and vigilance because you're not a little kid anymore. You've got a real adversary, the devil, who is walking about, in active search for someone to devour; like one of the lions on the Discovery Channel.

It just sounds to me like you God opened up some opportunities, filled in some gaps, put you in a different environment and that you got caught up in it all. It happens. It's happened to me but you can't be ready for some lion if you're drunk or not circumspect in your thinking but still walking. I'm hammering in this point Moses, because you've got to begin to steadfastly resist in your faith. It used to be seasonal attacks—asthma one year, masturbation another, musical theatre conflicts the next, your house another, grades another, disobedience another—but now, you're man enough and man enough in Christ for God to allow you to go through some things simultaneously and continually.

It's like getting a flu shot. You get the flu vaccine three months before the onslaught of the pronounced "flu season" so that your body can build up defenses and resistance against the flu by the time its season comes around. That's what God is doing in you.

This season is to build up your resistance for things that the enemy has planned, plotted and set in motion to happen years from now. But resistance isn't *how* you stand but that when attacked, if knocked out or you fall down or you straight up miss it all together, that you get back up and are ready in your mind for the next attack.

So again, Mo-Mo, (do they still call you that?), four words-two phrases, "Be Sober. Be Vigilant." And man you gotta resist your enemy. You're not just the only one going through stuff like this. The same tests you're going through and are passing are being experienced by your Christian brothers all over this world. (You know I like to write books but I seriously didn't plan for this one to be this long. Sorry.)

Two words again, my last words: "Benedict early." Mo' Better, after this trial or these trials or whatever you're going through, you will truly be "mo' better." "Benedict early" means pronounce a benediction over this trial even if it gets worst tomorrow and even worst next month. After you have gone through your "go through" and suffered a while, it is then that Jehovah, the God of all grace, who has <u>called</u> both you and me to his eternal glory by Christ Jesus, promises to make you complete and perfect; and to confirm, strengthen and settle you."

Benedict early,

Robin Peter Paul

There are times in a man's life when he needs his dad more than at other times. When his soul daily writes letters of communion and fellowship...when there is more hankering for friendship than a parent-child relationship. I wrote this letter to my dad one day in May. I call it,

<u>MAYDAY!</u> One is Enough

Dear Dad:
Today I asked God to give me the opportunity to give Him back all you had given me.

Today, still...in my state of becoming, I asked God to make me more like you; to give me the foresight to choose a woman who would love me forever and to stand with me no matter what; to give me the ability to displace my every fear before my family and to stand before them in all godliness and goodness, quiet power and subtle, almost cunning strength.

I asked God to do in my life what He had in yours—let me live the realization of my inner desire. Desire (to me right now) is more powerful than purpose. Desire gets you there... to the intersection where His plan, destiny and purpose all come together.

Dad, this letter is your faith document. This is the title deed to let you know that I've seen me better than where I am. I've seen you better than where you are and I've seen our family stronger, whole and occupying our perfect purpose as never before.

You lived as a man before me. The challenge of this season of my life is to put away my childish thoughts and understanding. T.D. Jakes taught me that it's not that I am saying that the things and thoughts of childhood are no longer enjoyable and that they must change, but that, to become the man GOD has for me and that I even have for myself, I must, even while enjoying what I enjoy, "put 'em away." They are not of where I am going but of where I am have been. I have to do this now so that I can get to live out my portion of, "but when I became a man." You did it so well. But I am tonight, at 9:10 PM, still...in my state of becoming.

In the state of my becoming [from child to man], I promise you I won't bring shame to the good name that you've given me. This man thing is harder than I thought. In the state of my becoming, I promise you that I will befriend you. That I may be a partaker of the same anointing and grace on your life as provider, I will sow into your life.

I promise you that I will rise up in your stead and do all that social times, economic hardships and timing denied you. I promise you...I will have, period. I will have and with all I have I'll make sure I have "understanding" along side of it.

I think you know as well as I that I was born a performer, a singer...

I never finished it. Life happened. Reader, whatever you started that was never completed because life happened, in most cases, it's not too late. Just pick up from the moment where God allowed life to interrupt you and sow into finishing the knowledge and emotion of the incomplete work within you. Either that or realize that life's interruptions are God's subtle ways of telling you, "It's perfect as it is. Present it to Me." Let the Church say, "Done-done."

when home HAS TO
get out of the exile place

CHAPTER 3

Confrontations in the exile place are designed to
make you *approach, one, subjects in this new place—*
especially the lifelong familiar friend known as your heart—
and two, every thing that happened subjectively against your
will in childhood and development.

Springing forth in this place is a personal agency all your own—
and not out of anyone's conditioning.
Your God is your God because it's just you and Him.
The wrestling match far from over, you begin to cling to Him
because you no longer have home, (in representation, reality or
even in heart) to count on. You're not supposed to.
For the first time in life, you realize that there is purpose in
being alone.

God leaves you alone until you realize that there is purpose in
that place.

To get home out I had to get to the exile place.
In the exile place, I began to set this boundary for me and me
only: "enough is enough."

You may have never heard this cry, but I walked and wrote
and rode in it.

1:15 Sunday July 16th, 2000
(what it is to be tired)

I'm tired of having to write but never being allowed to live
I'm ready to live comedies and not have to always write dramas.

I'm tired of having to deal with consequences and much fall-out of stuff I had nothing to do with. I didn't ask to be molested, I didn't invite being molested and I didn't want to be molested but that event, those events have set in motion the creation of a being within me which is not me.

I'm angry. This being is angry. I've taught myself how to camouflage it but I am angry. I am angry that I am because of it. I am not strong, I am not athletic...and I want to be, but this is as strong and as athletic as this being lets me be. I am not trusting and now even more suspicious of everything and everyone.

I see life, mine, as that of a eunuch. I am emasculated in everything I do. Anything too feminine I stay away from and anything too masculine I stay away from. I'm just moses. Not strong Moses, not tall Moses, not good at anything other than thinking...and writing but what manly-man gets praised for those things. I have the perception of myself as a eunuch but the heart of a man who doesn't understand.

I want to be stronger than this. I want to be stronger in the spirit of my mind. And my God how I want love and want to be loved. I want a female someone to find safety in me but I am so scared of me, of the anger in me that I shun the very appearance of the things and the people I need most. I understand me. I need You to create a creature who will love me even as I articulate who I am, interpret why I give off what I give off and speak of what really is the who of my actions.

Is it possible to be angry for 23 years? I don't want a girlfriend; she doesn't deserve to see me like this...still angry. She didn't do it and doesn't deserve to be the 2nd generation of fall-out because of my anger. The behavior from being angry and not understanding why has the power to set you up to be robbed of God's most choice blessing. I already know.

I have hit walls. I have hit steering wheels. I have thrown a briefcase at a wall and I have thrown a brother around such that I have knocked the door off its frame and also in a moemeant, have needed someone out my presence right then, right there that I have slammed a door in such a way that I've had light ornaments fall from their own security onto the person who came into the land of my anger. This is not because I am in a foreign land; this is because I have a foreign heart growing alongside mine. I didn't ask to be molested, I didn't invite being molested and I didn't want to be molested. I (tears falls) have lost all sense of inner balance and sense of inner strength. And the place where I felt safest, sanctuary, reportedly the head of that has even said that my praise and my worship are not even in order, not welcomed anymore. And the new place where I feel most revived, sanctuary, the head of it tells me he's proud of me but...where am I going with this?

I am an angry soul. And I am asking for help. I would rather not be married than to be married and be an angry soul and be this angry. If the only place you've ever received commendation and true promotion rejects any or all parts of you, where do you go?

What? I'm not good enough anymore. What? The truth of me dealing with my raggedy heart isn't good enough to lead your people into the inner court. But I thought worship was to be done in spirit and truth. I haven't held back that I need help; so why the demotion?

I don't want to die anymore. But, I do want this little thing in me that keeps loaning part of its heart out to others out of me. I want to trust. I want to trust...again. I believe in God and I believe in my mother and I believe in my father and I believe in my brothers and in my favorite sister, (I only have one), but as used of God as I am and as powerful as I can be in His spirit at times, I don't believe in myself. I don't believe in my ability to be anything but deep and a writer. But that's not enough. One day God will fill this void and I won't have anything about which to write. Although I'm tired of writing dramas and want to live some seasons of comedy, the day is coming when I will have run the tap dry and will be without. What then will be me?

If I don't write how will I get in touch with God? If I don't write, what will I have to give to him? What will be my offering? I can't give Him my heart because it's not fully mine. (That's why I'm not in a relationship because my heart is not fully mine. I know the slow cancer within and refuse to contaminate another.) I am not that angry because God has been too good. So if what I had was praise and worship, and man demoted me from giving that out and if I get to the day when I have nothing else to be deep about or write about, where will Moses be?

I am a 26-year-old man still angry with God about something that happened to me 23 and 15 years before I gained voice to voice the memories, icky feelings and lies told to me so I would just let thim touch me. I am too old to begin crying myself to sleep again. Been there, done that. I am about to become 27 years old in less than a month and as it relates to friendships and interpersonal communication, I live my experience out of the diseased-imparted heart and not the pure one God gave me. But age 27 won't let me bring ...[tears, emotional breakdown and breakthrough]... "Oh God, please change me; oh God, please change me, Oh God please change me, please change me." I don't want to be promoted, I want this diseased portion of my heart that trusts the wrong people and won't say no even when it's hurting me out of me. I can't raise sons for your kingdom like this. They'll end up like me. Being me in 2000 is fine but being me in 2028 is death. Please God, today, at 1:46 PM change me. I am a prodigal son now in a place You have confirmed you exiled me to but my heart is not even of my home. My heart is back in nursery school. My voice is back in nursery school. My power is back in naptime. I don't want to be like this. I will self-destruct by my self, everything good and Godly thing you give me with a heart like this.

I don't want to beat anyone down. I don't want to beat anyone down, I just want peace. I hear Ce Ce in the background singing, *"Where there is peace, there will be hope."* I am a survivor but my soul and its anger has survived too. One of us has to die. It's not even a choice anymore. in this land of exile, before i take a wife and build my family, i will rebuild myself. i will slay the anger within. You've done enough. You didn't molest me; he did through those two men. "Spirit of anger and your lineage, your a_ _ es are mine," he said in righteous indignation.

1:55 pm

before little boy hearts get grown

July 5, 2000
8:35 pm

I look at all my fathers.
None of them aged like Shirley, Tina or even Tommy.
They age and die because of what they sowed while they still were
working out and <u>through</u> their little boy hearts.

I look at all my fathers.
Whoosh!
Is it too late...for me.?
Have I sown too much since my first fall?

Theirs cannot be what is pre'd for me.
What lesson.
What more must I go through?
Who else must I know and be left behind by?
Who else must I watch suffer in the holiest of earth's institute's—
barren, shamed for things my fathers did even before together
they came?

My first father died
My second father has barrenness as his male child
And I am next
In line for what? Will there even be a mine to hold or "of mine"
to behold?
And my brothers, we share the same blood but have no power.

i dream of Ichabod webs

I woke up this morning to a strange sight.
A web in the corner of the pen.
One word intricately displayed, "ICHABOD"
What does it mean?
As I looked at it I thought to myself, "how did I live, what choice did I make that gave me the "I" which took all glory out of my life?"...And now I live in a pen, nothing play about it."

I woke up this morning to a strange vision.
I saw one pig situated on another; but this pig's hind parts were on another's snout. (Was is it a dream, reality, a memory of something I saw in my father's house or something I always wanted to see...or did I really see that at all?) What kind of mess is that? But I guess as such is the nature of pigs, the more they struggled to move, (and I saw the one, no, both of them struggle to change positions), the dirtier they got. Mm.

There was an alliance between Boss Hog (that one pig from a while back who was sitting on the snout of that other pig) that I just stumbled upon. Now as for the alliance between Boss Hog and his confederate, Duke, (man, how that hog was hazardous to all of us in here), that partnership is over. Citizen Cain, the far-country farmer who allows me to stay here, in the hog-pen, for free, rose early one morning and took Duke to the market; that was just weeks ago.

Mm. I woke up this morning to a sight. Boss Hog was sitting on <u>my</u> face! Don't laugh. I am a man, but awoke to a pig lying on my face. Who ever heard of a pig even lounging that comfortably with a human? I mean, I know I have been in this hog pen now a little longer than a while and that *I* am the foreigner, (I mean I do know it is a "hog-pen" and by definition anyone who lives in one should be wholly hog), but has my identity become so indistinguishable that Boss Hog saw me, even in the remotest sense, like him? I could take waking up with egg on my face; we all go through seasons or experiences of embarrassment. This isn't embarrassment. I woke up and there is a pig on my face.

Woke up this morning. Boss Hog had some different kind of mire on him. Any time Citizen Cain lets him out to other farmers he comes back different. He had the essence of essowinancy all over him. Oink.

Mornin'. Saw something. I looked up and saw the firmament while my arms were around Boss Hog. A man does many a strange thing when he misses home and a stretch of independence (but not self-sufficiency) has made pen-sive living home. Sketched in the corner of the pen where my head laid was, "Consider your dereks."

Derek...that's my younger brother. Not my brother, what's happned to my brother! Greenville, what does that mean?! "Consider my younger brothers?" Oink. What ways do I have that don't allow me to punt this skin clear out of my, this stadium. But wait a minute, *I'm* the one out of position. I can't fault Boss Hog for being pig.

I know Boss Hog is fully pig but at times, for whatever reason, (and I cannot explain it), he reminds me of Garrett, my brother who drowned in the red sea. Garrett Raphael, Raafi. So though he's not G., it's like Boss Hog has purpose, like he fills Raafi's place. I want to call him Raafi II, ya know? It's like God's given me my brother back. Mm. He's not my brother but is God given so I'll call him my cousin. No, my God brother.

But he's not a God brother.

He's not a God brother. He's not Raafi.

He's not a God brother

And I heard others...of my hometown often say, "Oh this [pig] is my God brother" or "This [hog] is my Uncle Rocky" or "This is my cousin or my mentee," (essowinate as the day is long), "Li'l Piggly." Back then I always questioned it, but it can't even be raised as a question with me and Boss Hog 'cause I know my heart. (My heart: I just miss Raafi and no one allows me to talk about it. No one even acknowledges he existed and it's been thirty years.) And by God, once, I met the Notorious P.I.G.: a great, big, dark-skinned, street-smart, hustling Godfather Pigger. This pastor wore the mask of a spiritual father but all of his little *sons*, his piglets in the ministry, were prostituted according to their areas of struggle. "Drug distribution on 14th, pick it up!" "Homosexuality downtown, pick it up!"

But Boss Hog is not Raafi.

He's not my brother,

not my father,

not my Godfather,

not my God brother,

not my mentor,

not my mentee,

not my disciple,

not my father in the ministry,

not my son in the ministry,

not a Barnabas to my Paul,

not a Paul to my Barnabas

not a Timothy to my Paul

and not a Paul to my Timothy.

Not my cousin-first, second or third.

He is a hog and hogs and men don't mix; at least not as Divinely recognized and approved.

Boss Hog is wholly pork. Before I came to this hog pen he was wholly pork so what am I waiting for? For this pig to be delivered from being a pig? That's not deliverance... that's...just not deliverance .

I'm trying to come to myself. My wisdom is telling me, "MOVE ON." Move on in heart, move on in action, move on in purpose, and move on into my destiny. Not necessarily to move back to Jerusalem but to move on. I wonder what dad is doing. I wonder if he's even thinking about me. Or Raafi.

Greenville is dead. Her last web said, "No One Cavity?"

I've come to myself. My entire life has become a cavity. My life is no one's cavity. Being created as a man, I am a producer by design, not a receptacle. And I was made from dust not mire so this whole environment is foreign to me. I'm not a receptacle of Boss Hog's mess; of his longing for others, for his past actions and present wants of who he is. And as for the citizen they call Cain...

It was foreign for me to walk even <u>one</u> <u>day</u> with Boss Hog and to receive any thing from him in any form was against the nature of things.

He's not Raafi.
He's not a God brother.
He's not a God brother.
He's not a God brother.
Hogs and *this* man don't mix; at least as divinely recognized and approved. Oink.

The most tremendous blessing of independence has become the most tremendous and most awesome deterrent of my destiny. I am independent of eating regularly. I am independent of peace of mind. I am independent of ministry. I am independent of self-respect, forget the respect of others but I don't even respect my self. I am independent of integrity and holiness as my testimony and I dwell in a place of heart (and experience of that same heart) called, "The Hogpen." And, I live in an environment of webs. Augh! Greenville and her great-great-great-grandmother Charlotte had nothing on this place!

I hated webs back home so you know how these webs must affect me. But, oink, they were familial and familiar webs; I knew how to deal with them. But the craftsmanship of the webs down here— I ain't never lived no thing like this in my life!

"Move me Lord. Prosper me from this place." Greenville's webs are right. I (in my living and in my pride) added the "I" to your "chabod." Greenville's webs are right I do have to consider my ways and my impact on my brothers. Greenville's webs are right, I am no one's cavity; not one's, no not one's.

Move me, Lord, from this place. Move me from this place, Lord. Move me from this place, Lord. It's not about my voice; it's about discernment. It's about calling hog "hog" and human "human." I discern that this is counterproductive, counter-everything to my ultimate purpose. I'm out. I've come to myself without a hand other than your hand on me. Move me, Lord.

"Move yourself." (For every action there is an equal or opposite reaction.) "You put forth the effort, you en-actioned your body to move from Me, move yourself."

"Wash me."

"You en-actioned an environment of much muck and mire, you now begin to scrub-a-dub-dub yourself back to the standard of uprightness, of a right-standing relationship with Me. Wash yourself."

Cleanse me?

"Cleanse yourself."

Encourage me? "

"Encourage yourself."

"I want to go home"

"Home is within yourself"

"I want to be made whole"

"Wholeness is within yourself. I am able. I AM able. But this time it's not about my ability. You left downtown Philadelphia for far country, further than yet exactly sub-urbane living. You've got to get back to a Main Street, City Hall lifestyle yourself. This time it will be you walking out MY ability in you that brings you not out or back or through but completely *to* Me. As your cousin Spikley used to say, "WAAAAAAAAAKE UUUUUUUUPPPPPPP!"

6/20/00 The Richest Man I Know

T is the richest man I know...and he lives with his wife and their daughters back in his parents' house.

T has been given a spirit to whom to be husband whose womanly encasement I have watched brothers on the yard & in the House envy. (It really should say "admire" and that they envy him). She She loves him. Period. I mean what man is poor when the very spirit of the beautiful rib given back to complete the work God created (in or for) him loves him.

Ahhhh, T is the richest man I know...and he lives with his wife and their daughters, two, of them, back in his parent's house.

Pining After The Then Place: A Trilogy

6/23/00 3:47 pm (LIFE-TIME RATION)

It's something. At 26, I am as strong, physically, as I ever thought I <u>would</u> be; not as I <u>wanted</u> to be but I am that in strength that I thought I would attain.

Sad, isn't it? I know that I will (be) more famous than I currently am. That's a knowledge. Time has to fulfill that for me. Fame is strength to me, not motivation; just part of my strength. Hmm. That's a thought. Not a revelation-just a thought. Do I not perceive myself as strong because I am without fame.

Just a thought. (That's why there is no question mark).

Fame isn't necessarily

5:45 pm 6/23/00 (DESPER RATION)

If you send her now, today, I promise YOU I'll cherish her for my lifetime.

Thought.

Not a "rescue 9-mo-mo" love. I don't need a savior.
Not a "here I come to save the day" love. I don't need to save, to be Mighty Mo-use (ouse)
I won't lie...it hurts too much, all the time, like a nagging migraine.
First, build <u>me</u> –this one hundred and–

June 28th or So (CRE-RATION)

I'm envisioning my rib right now.
What does she look like you ask? You tell me. All I can see is her heart.
Just got a 7:30 revelation. To start with complexion, size, figure, eyes shape, color, the length of her hair is to miss it from the beginning. How dare I start my request at the end of God's workmanship for surely the body he gives to encase the heart of the spirit I desire is his finishing touch. That's probably why guys can find an number of women to meet the specifications of a female's outer being or non being, (Non being speaks to the extras a woman can find to augment, alter her); and still not be satisfied.

So...first, if in the beginning was the Word, at the beginning of her spirit I want the Word. I want her to have a passion for God that ignites my pilot for Him, which is balanced by her sense and awareness of herself as God's child. No me involved. Who is she without me? Who is she before me, before I even enter the picture? Do you know a woman like this?

Stay with her spirit. I...No, go to her heart.

I want a woman to have a heart like God describes David's: ruddy, of a beautiful countenance and goodly to look to. My revelation. I'm getting stuck because I'm afraid to say what I want, what I see for myself, not because of me, and maybe not because of you, but possibly because it seems too much.

Her heart is as beautiful as she is. Her outward beauty is a mirror of her spirit and of the work God alone has done in her heart. She has quiet, reserved strength...like my dad.

[Got interrupted...at DC Hand-Dancing class. Write later.]

10:57
Thoughts of a train ride home

I would give one million dollars to be back home right now. I would give three million to be back in my old bedroom, pretending I was sleep when my daddy came in from his nighttime job, just so I could act like his coming in woke me and say, "Hey dad!" He'd have Carvel soft ice cream and Dunkin Donuts (on the weekend) or a vanilla shake with nuts and crushed pineapples and wouldn't let me or my brother use his straw but would give us a spoonful of all that good stuff down at the bottom. Yeah, that's worth three million.

I would give one million dollars for one day of my childhood. A million to make a cake with my mom and my brother Derek Saturday night before having to go take a bath. No, I'd really give four million to make rolls with mom Saturday night. She would always let me steal some dough. In the midst of it dad would call me upstairs to write out my $1.00 tithe envelope and then make me take my bath.

I would. One day of dad taking me to Buster Brown for new Sunday shoes or to Modell's where there was this table top that had all these same kind of boots in different sizes still attached by a little plastic something-or-other that you couldn't take off and me and Derek would have to try on these shoes, sneakers and boots...and somehow walk in them. That's worth a mill.

Two million for a Saturday afternoon ride to the church for mom's choir rehearsal and then to Farmer's Market for kosher pickles and grease-flowing pizza from the man who was set up right across from the people whom mom bought her pantyhoses from. There we would see the saints. We see the people who we always saw.

I would give a million to have one day being back in my house. In my room.

**statutory
psalm**

CHAPTER 4

Music for Through the Roof Music Unlimited, Inc. Country & Western with much gospel strain and twang and the desperation of blues of Psalm 42 and 43. In the tradition of Conway Twitty and Dolly Parton.
10:45 PM March 20, 2000

how many times will psalm 51 be my song?

VERSE I

LORD, *how many times will David's sin be my own?*
And his CHOICES *be played out in my ways?*
LORD, I'M SO SORRY *that I am back at your throne with the same repentive song...*

CHORUS

Oh Lord, how often will I come to you singing PSALM 51,
my heart can't take it no more
Oh Lord how many times in one day will I have to come and ask you
Won't you cleanse me, forgive me, once more and again
Lord, please cleanse me and forgive me again

VERSE II

FATHER, *there's a law within me that is upheld without end,*
Flesh is burning, soul soon to follow if you don't rescue me...
That which I desire to do, I do not but all of those things I really don't want to do—
I do with great pleasure THAT IS AT THE TIME
How long before I become reprobate in my mind?

CHORUS:

Oh Lord, how often will I come to you singing PSALM 51,
my heart can't take it no more
Oh Lord how many times in one day will I have to come and ask
you
Won't you cleanse me, forgive me, once more and again
Lord please cleanse me and forgive me again

ALL SPOKEN:

I MET A PASTOR FROM OREGON AND I ASKED HIM, "HOW
LONG WILL I KEEP SINGING THIS SAME OLE PSALM TO THE
LORD? AND IN <u>HIS</u> ANSWER...
(Sungwith great truth-sung) Lord, I saw and heard you and alllll
of Your love,
When he said, "MOSES, until you get it right."
 (BREAK—sounds of trickling of rain then the rushing, fury
of the crashing of a waterfall.....)RAISE KEY

USE MELODY OF CHORUS:

So Lord, I am coming to You once more and again to (get Gospel)
say-ay-ay
Psalm 51 is where I am let me find your love right there
Can't make a joyful noise or even clap my hands because guilt and
anguish desire to ravish my soul, Won't you help please, come on
down and rescue me I don't want to stay so long that you turn me
over to this.

Won't you cleanse me, forgive me once more and again

Lord please cleanse me and forgive me once more, once more, once more, once more, once more,
Once more once more, Lord one more time, Let me not have frustrated your grace Lord
Forgive me and cleanse me once (ritard) more and again
Lord....(broken voice) ....please ...(music continues) (real breathy— the desperation of the plea) Please.

The End

Hallelujah!!

NIGHTshock

CHAPTER 5

*It is your unrehearsed reactions to the surprises of life
that provide the strongest evidence for or against your witness.
Do you trust Him as your Sovereign God or not?*

Praise & Worship's Usher
written a June 23rd Morning

If you can lead praise and worship when you are hurting then you can do any thing. That's what my mom taught me and Maya, Oprah. If you can say "thank you" when it hurts the most...If you, in the moment, can exalt Jesus above your pain, then you have experienced praise and worship.

Picture it: every other Sunday for over two years I was responsible for leading our congregation into "that time of the service." There is nothing, no thing, glamorous about praise and worship, with leading, especially. With leading especially.

Picture more: I will never forget the Father's love and acceptance of my own personal praise and worship on this one particular Sunday.

From my seat in the musicians' corner I can see every thing and every one in the entire congregation, besides let's say, one-eighth of the people. My role in service, my role in life is that of a praise and worship leader and choir director. Positioned, in service and in life, to intercede for those in, around and under my care. My job description (if I had one there) would have included:

    a. Must intercede through song for the successful sowing of the pastor's message;

    b. Must intercede through worship for the entire congregation; and,

    c. Must do spiritual, unseen and unimaginable warfare for them-all of them, them all, all.

On this "Picture more-particular Sunday," soon after I enter I begin to do what I have trained myself to do. I look around the place called "The Sanctuary," surveying it like a general or a spy before I open my mouth and spirit to say one thing. The deacons are devotioning, the Zenos zenoing, the choir choiring and me, I'm warfaring.

Normally, if something is up, God tells me. But when I was a child, He pre-prepared me for every twist and turn like a child. Well, I was, at that time, in my state of becoming; still am. But this day, without advanced notice, my eyes see an enemy. She's here. Whoosh! Okay, I gotta get it together. I have to have it together. Thank God my mother's late. But, I gotta save her heart. God is able but I am tangible.

I look left. My mother's sisters are in the choir, my choir. The reality is that I am on stage. People there, in the choir and within the place called "the sanctuary" already know what's up. (Listen, most times when sin has abounded, most times, it and the knowledge of it has never stayed between the two people involved. Sometimes Grace is sanity found through a listening ear.) So I go to write a letter because mouthing my reality to my aunts in front of my choir will alert the hyenas that I am fazed. I try anyway, to no avail.

My mom. I've gotta get to her. No! I'm within the place; some call it "the sanctuary." Right now, it is an all out war zone; and *blessed* walks in. She sings in the choir all the way on the other side. The very side facing the other woman.

I can't see my mom because of a potted plant. When I finally get her to look at me, she thinks I'm telling her something about her robe or her hair; nothing about the surprise heart attack that is about to hit the Shores.

Offering. I don't remember which choir was singing or why I was distracted, but it happened. She knew I know. There is a knowledge that exists between a mother and her child that transcends the cut of the umbilical. It is communicated in the eyes. I've heard that the enemy imparts through whatever body-gates are available. I won't speak on that. But, I *can* say that God imparted an exchange of Strength, virtue and understanding between my mother and I this day; and neither of us even left our seats.

Mom became mom. mom bear, mom lioness, thespiana mama. It is innate. There is a surge of Heaven and testosterone that crashes up when a woman sees the woman who tried...and her children are close by. Even being in the sanctuary, a place she has known before, doesn't stop this mighty rushing wind. She looked to her sisters.

Oh God. They are reading the Scripture. I'm not ready. I was, but- ...With everyone watching her was anyone interceding for me?

If you can lead praise and worship when you are hurting then you can do any thing. If you can lead others into the Throne room of God—past the point of your own pain—you've become the essence of Gethsemane. Geth-semen-knee. That's how I'll survive the calling of this moment and Betty knows it. She taught us to do what they teach you in elementary school in case of a fire, pray. I don't have to physically get on my knees right now but my heart is prostrate, one with the crimson-colored carpet camouflaging the Rock Who is keeping my feet.

Okay, I'm up and my normal character time has been wasted preparing others.

I take the microphone. Real is what I am in my praise. If I purpose not to look at her then I've stopped up my ministry. Whoosh. (I don't remember the song I sang, but I know it had to have been medium tempo to upbeat. Though "Jesus Keep Me Near The Cross" is my prayer, my heart can't take four verses of anything that slow. The blood in my own heart has to move.)

Well, I decide to look in the direction of the woman. Hey, you know me. I'm 23, old enough to look anything in the eye. My heart fails me. Not because of her, although this is my first time seeing her since I was 18, on Christmas break, when she came down the aisle of the toy store where I was working with her husband. Quickly walk back to Aisle 2 with me.

It was my first time seeing her in years. And we spoke. Friendly, and back then a super-saint, super-believer that everyone at the Church loved me and my family and lived holy, I probably initiated the conversation. I know I did. Torturing the spirit of the enemywithout even knowing it. Mm. I hate conversations that are not even, not pure. It's not even the meta. It's wrong. It's sin and evil camouflaged as happenstance. It's a set up.

Backstory segue: I still remember coming home the day I saw her in the aisle. It was either Christmas Eve or New Year's. It was Christmas Eve because my favorite uncle and aunt and cousins were over for our holiday season tradition. I walked into the kitchen where my aunt, non-blood, and mother were and said, "Hey mom! Guess who I saw at my job today?" Then I spoke a reality I had yet to become a part of ...consciously. There was this look my mom gave my aunt. "What happened?" I asked.

Thespiana mama bear and Thespianissa auntie bear dismissed my intuition that my words had triggered something. The cougar had not only gotten close enough to the cub to kill it, but had paraded a ½ cougar ½ bear in front of it. "...And she had this cute little boy with her."

Real time: Stunned. Machine stun-gunned. My heart is failing me because I see eyelashes, mine. As a little boy I was always known by and complimented for having these long, beautiful eyelashes. The woman and I caught eyes. She looked down. Sitting next to her in the sanctuary was me in Toys R Us five years earlier; someone else oblivious to truth, even in a place called "The Sanctuary." If you can lead praise and worship when you are hurting then you can do anything. If you can sing and not appear jilted to men although you are Samson slaying thousands of emotions with the jawbone of an ass, qualified are you.

I had never seen him before, just heard stories (much like tales and fables) for five years. I was away in school. I was away in school. I was away from my brother. I was away from my sister. I was away from my other brother. They were in school.

I remember the morning mom told me. She and I were on our way to the 5:25 a.m. Sunday morning service at my college church, The Gates Of Hell Shall Not Prevail Against Zion Evangelical Holiness Church in Southwest Nazareth. (Try writing all of that on your check for tithes!) TGOHSNPAZEHC only had room enough for thirty people in the main sanctuary and each of the four overflow rooms could only hold six small people so we had to hold twelve services each Sunday from 5:25 a.m. to 5:35 p.m. and as part of the choir, I had to sing at all of them.

As it was a forty-minute drive from my house in the suburbs to the church I can't say that I remember how mom started the conversation. I know his age surprised me. Only two years younger than us. Wait, *I* was dating. I was in what grade! I reckon I never saw anything like this cougar-bear stuff on the Discovery Channel. But I don't remember what she said. In moments when what you have believed to be your reality vaporizes into desert dew at best, and the present burning kindling is that hell's fires have infiltrated your kindred, your ark of safety, your nu'ahch, I'm not sure if you remember what words are actually used to communicate the shift. I think that's God's grace on the mind.

After mom told me the truth, I had, maybe two blocks before we got to the church. Mom went in the front door and I went through the back entrance for the choir members. Dax, one of my closest college friends was just as late as I was so I at least had the opportunity to have someone hear my faint cry before combustion. Sometimes grace is sanity found through a listening ear.

I had to get the pain off of me. I didn't want to make sense of what my mother had just told me. You can't make sense of that which defies your perception of sense. I believe all I told Dax was, "Pray for me and for my family."

Whether praise was in the building or I brought in a need to praise the sovereignty of God's will and plans I know not. "Don't hit that key, Twinkie!" I was gone!

And I didn't apologize. In the past, there were times that I did. But today, this morning of my college years, if you wanted me to apologize, "Go to hell. Go directly to hell. Do not pass 'Go!' Do not collect $200." I wasn't cussin' anyone out, but I needed him or her and/or you to understand that hell was what was making me praise God like this. Hell had descended upon my life. My words were a dare for that man or Michal who even so much as looked for an apology from me to have hell enter their life at such an unsuspecting time—right before a scheduled time for service, ministry and worship before the Father—that they felt their destiny had been altered and then see, if either of them had time to concentrate on my praise such that he or she, individually or collectively could form lips to say, "It don't take all of that, brother!" Hallelujah! My words were given to say, if it took a little bit of hell for a quencher of my praise to shut his or her mouth and understand that if I didn't praise God in the only place that there is supposed be safety, "His Sanctuary" then they needed to go to hell; not to stay, just to pass through.

No one knew the conversation that brought the "I've got to praise God right now unabashedly!"-praise out of me; or the "If I don't get this 'Hallelujah' out in spite of my shipwrecked situation the capacity is in me to pick up a knife"-uplifted hands out of me; or the "if I don't dance a 'thank YOU although I don't understand why, but I will not try to bear this by myself"-cry out of me. Hear me: if you can muster up and will yourself to say, "Yes, Lord" having been broad-sided by news that you've been living at 10 while your mother, father, brother, sister and other brother have been dealing back at zero, you are in line for a well done.

Real time (-with mom, aunts and sister): Not focusing on but also not acting oblivious to the cougar and ½ cougar ½ bear in the pews facing me, I led my home church back in Babylon into the Place. The congregation danced. The congregation praised. The congregation kind of worshipped. They were able to dance, praise and kind of worship then because two years earlier, off a Twinkie-note and a capsized reality, I had managed to switch to my reserve gas tank and dance and worship my God even though I had just walked in the knowledge of a decade old secret. Had I not worshipped back then I would have exploded in front of the congregation *this* Sunday morning. Thanks for the vaccination, Lord.

But you could tell it wasn't enough. Pastor wanted more. He sat, musing in the spirit. The Spirit "died down" (I hate that terminology) and mom stepped forward. "No, Betty Faye! No! I've satisfied the bread ration for the day. No mom! We, you...we don't have to prove any thing! Mom!"

Without one instrument in her immediate coattail she praised. She had interceded for me during the praise and worship segment to lead the people into the holy of holies. A level of that now satisfied, she would be the one to explode if she herself didn't praise Him; if for nothing else than the fact that I didn't crack up in front of Jerusalem.

A dance wouldn't get it out. Therefore, she opened her spirit.

If you can by God's grace lead praise and worship after you have had to intercede for your oldest born son who has seen the woman who physically embodied the mind of the serpent in co-mingling with your Adam, his dad; the same son who is just seconds out of the tranquilizer of praise having been the only panacea for the shock of seeing his half-brother for the first real time, a previously unbeheld portion of his father's strength; and this very son has still been required by God and man to put the knowledge of this to the side and lead over five hundred people into the holy of holies~ one-third of whom know the secret and are looking for a reaction, then you can do anything!

Mom sang, "He's an on-time God, yes he is."

At first I thought she was out of order; that there was no need. (I had even seen *this* portion in a dream earlier in the year and remembered crying out, "No, ma, no!") But I was able to be because she was. When I walked into this understanding, I cheered her, openly. The other woman even stood up to praise her God. At first, I was appalled, but in a week I realized who was I to judge.

Then, the Church *really* praised. Then the Church *really* danced. Then....the Church *really* entered in. We got beyond the veil.

I don't know how to end this story. This experience will NEVER end—it's alive through my brother. But reader resolve to know this: if you can find the strength to give God a word of praise or a "thank you" in the midst of a sudden change in your perceived reality; when you have bought into a lie and the lie's lie enters your inner or outward place of sanctuary, and you still can sing like nobody's business, and people, even the one who was used to facilitate your pain, their pain and the supposed demise of you and yours, stands to his or her feet and he or she is even equipped to praise your God, in that instance you have arrived or been, like me, exiled from Jerusalem (the founded peaceful place) to Babylon (the place of much mindless muttering) but are also so anointed that GOD can now honor you with a commendation: "The I AM hereby bestows [PUT YOUR NAME HERE], to have fulfilled and satisfied the requirements of John 4:24." God calls you *His* worshipper.

What has led me and my mom and now my sister into

A MIGHTY GLORY CAME OVER ME. HAD TO PRAISE. YOU READ THIS AGAIN. IT IS NOT THE INCIDENT THAT LED, THAT PROMOTED US AS PRAISE AND WORSHIP AND INNER COURT LEADERS. It is PAIN: Pain & Hurt. The SUDDEN surprise...life-rocking realities

GLORY CAME AGAIN

DONE DONE. Not supposed to write more. You are at the threshold: Behold The Lamb.

...Sometime before

What's your name? Thomas. Look Thomas, how much do you make here? I can't tell you that. Do you make enough to make cover your monthly bills? No. How much do you need to cover your bills? $1300...Thomas, listen man, come work with me. Do everything I say and if you don't make $1300 back in that one month, I promise I will give it to you...

Sometime *before* before...

Warren, this store needs something else. You know we sell out of every suit-shirt-tie combination that I create. Can I at least design the looks for the mannequins? Thomas, we hired you just to sell clothing. Thomas, I need you to watch the store. Thomas, look there's a customer right there...

...Warrenton, what's going on with my benefits? It's been four months. You don't work for any company, no matter how new they are to the market, and not know if you have benefits. White folk don't be going through this!...Thomas, call Kansas City yourself. I don't know what's going on.

...Sometime before sometime *before* before

War, what's going on with my paycheck? The changes are still not reflected. Thomas, I've been meaning to tell you. This store is not like the old store. Although I am in the same position I was in at the old store, the owners gave me a salary cap for my employees. I am not going to be able to pay you what I promised you in your interview. What!

frustrated until the mirage shows pyramids: not on paper

7:19 **A month after the first before**

I don't know if I'd call it fear or not, but something is happening to me. I don't like this atmosphere. I don't understand it. My stomach is turning and my heart is hollow and I'm just not used to this. It's not a fear of money. This...millionaires, (probably 2%, no .5% and 99.5% wanna-be-millionaires), is NOT my environment. Have I just crossed into a place no one in my family has before or is this a familiar place but mom and dad just didn't become acclimated to it?

My stomach is sick and my heart is palpitating, racing. I've never known unfamiliarity like this. NEVER. This is a new fear. I don't feel like I belong here. I don't feel most people really <u>are</u> where they (are) or where I am projecting them to project themselves as being.

They look too perfect. Things are too polished. Is this God or satan polished to be divine? I'm scared. Two days delivered by the Word through Deron Cloud I won't walk and take the bait of satan to bind me up all over again.

I won't clap because I don't like this whole groupthink thing. They repeat his words, they all envy him and want to be him. That's not me. I'm satisfied with myself. I just need to be financially valued for the gifts and talents God's given me. I quiet myself to hear the voice of God. He chants like he is a preacher.

He sounds too programmed. Like his sermon is too together. But he sounds like a true witness. If I sounded like this when I preached I would deliver many souls.

He is too polished. So I'm here in faith. Fear. So I'll sell in faith. I'll walk, in faith, into wealth, into black wealth...in faith. I'll be a transitional person. I'll be the transitional person of wealth with integrity, praise & worship and a standard of holy living in my family.

They're chanting, "Money Cometh!" I don't want it without You coming before it, You coming with it, You coming wrapped up in it. I need money to come towards me, to me, but I need You, Lord. Lord, I need You and bring riches and prosperity with You.

"...As children of God it is your birthright to prosper." But how?

...A month after the first before: When many a true thing was said: Ingest

"Did you...or did you....how many...and how many times ....have you...when did you? But you said. ...What! Man, if you think I'm going to give you thirteen hundred dollars, you crazy!"

The immediate non-moemeant reflection that followed a month after the first before; when many a thing was said: Ingest

Money cometh! ...As children of God it is your birthright to prosper. But how?
Money cometh! ...it is your birthright to prosper. But how?
Money cometh! But how?
Money- but how?
Mo- but how?

Go back to S.S.; Sunday School or Sesame Street, doesn't matter.

H

URT

HURT

WH

EN

WHEN

N

OT

NOT

WR

ITTEN

WRITTEN

Money cometh!

But how?

ON PAPER

Corinthia's Day + Opportunity Cost =Altered Destiny

I want to send these words sooner than later. I've already heard words and buzzes of "What's going on with Thomas?" "Where was Byrd?" and, "Cori was greatly disappointed and hurt that Thomas didn't show."

Because of the nature of the truth, I would appreciate it if you and Sonny shared in this alone and not with everyone who is asking what happened to me. The truth is for you because you deserve to hear it.

See my heart. It too has hurt and been disappointed in the fact that I couldn't make your wedding. Please know that it was not purposed. Know that I had no idea up until late Thursday evening before the Saturday before your wedding that my reality was that I could not make it. If you remember, your wedding was something about which you and I had emailed one another often. In private, I had been asking God to bless His presence with since I received the first email from you and Sonny after last year's choir anniversary.

See my heart. Look past what seems apparent in my actions and past every impression that people or even your own heart has given you. See my heart and hear the truth.

Cori, I recently took a financial risk, made a financial investment of sorts that didn't pay off. The decision put me close to bankruptcy. Plan B was to sell my car and use the profit to cover my debt and ride with Shawn and Lia (as they had offered me a ride to your wedding). The profit from selling my car was to finance my way back from the wedding. There was a $5,000 difference in the price quoted to me over the phone for Isaac and that which was offered in person. Yes, Shawn and Lia offered a ride but my reality was that I didn't have enough financial resources to get back to Babylon; especially as I had an almost $3,000.00 legal obligation due the Tuesday after your wedding.

Be me. Do I spend my last to go to a friend's wedding that I really want to be at without any assurance that I will be able to cover that which I spent to get there and make a profit such that I won't be in a worse off financial position after I get back? It's Thursday night (about 11 PM) and the dealer didn't buy Isaac. Do I call Cori or try to call her sister Mavis back in Jerusalem and explain what has happened? The wise counsel I sought instructed me that the day before a woman's wedding, she is already a bit anxious. Therefore wait until after the wedding and then reveal your circumstances.

I am not a lover of money. I didn't *choose* to work Saturday in total disregard to my commitment of attending your wedding. Life chose this decision for me. This is the truth. Shawn and Lia were not lying or hiding any thing else. I had to work so that I wouldn't find myself on the street the very next week.

I have thought of your feelings and the perception you were sure to come away with all this past week. Corinthia...you know me. I sought wise counsel and I believe that I did what, because of some life choices I had made, I had to do. It was not an easy decision and not a decision based on my relationship with you and whether or not you would really miss my presence. It was a decision for my mere survival. I couldn't get money from even my most familiar sources as I would need their help in assisting me with my legal challenges and meeting my other immediate financial obligations.

I would enjoy the opportunity to talk to you over the phone. I am truly sorry if the lack of my presence offended you in any way or made you to believe that I don't love you. Every word I have written and said to you in the past regarding my admiration of your walk, your integrity and your very being as Corinthia Eva-Lynnette (Harrington) Kirubi I have meant.

My deepest regret is that a financial risk and decision I made months ago caused me to miss out in celebrating with someone as dear to my heart as you and who has meant so much in my spiritual growth.

Yours in truth and in Christ,

Thomas Kered Linquist a.k.a Byrd

when moses
comes to moses

CHAPTER 6

I remember one night. I just sat on the edge of the bathtub as the water ran and ran and the thought that irrigated my mind was, "Lord, I don't want to die or kill myself; I just want to go to sleep and come back tomorrow." Some time later someone knocked at the door. Listen. There are times in life when the pain, the weight is so unbearable that the only salvation is a knock at the door. Listen more closely for the water. Is there any one who sits on the edge? If so, with all your might, knock; they can come to themselves. That's a knock that's neither loud nor soft but one that allows the person to be on his or her cross in front of you. Put religion aside; knock with understanding. "Thanks, J."

Yellow Lady Bug on the 7:51 Train

No one ever
Makes the same allowances.
No one ever does.
No one ever
Makes the same allowances for me.
No one ever does.

What
Made
Moses
Not
Enter
In?

He made too many allowances.
When God spoke death
          and destruction
And even repented of the good toward them,
Moses put his life on the line...
For a people who just would
          NOT live out the miracle of The Exodus.
And it was because
He pleaded with
The Lord that they were still alive.

Alive enough to irritate his nerves such that
In anger,
          he who interceded,
          he who stood

in the gap for an entire nation,
He did not but only
See the place he was chosen to go into...
For himself, too, (as well as the selves),
He—smote the rock and God punished him,
        who interceded,
For not doing what was asked,
        a Kindergarten lesson,
        "speak, don't hit."
Someone else.

Someone else alive enough—
By the prayers of *my* mouth—
To cause that unchecked
        (and not easily provoked,
        just not completely worked out in me),
To cause me premature death.

No one else
Makes the same allowances for me.
No one ever does.
No one ever
Makes the same allowances
For <u>this</u> Moses.
No one ever does.

It's nothing more than a Brentwood soccer field lesson.
It's a lesson my dad,
        ha!—his name is Moses, too,
Tried to teach me; when he was my coach.

I was his halfback.
Or is that full back?
Whatever the position, I stood right in
Front of my dad's goal, no "s".

Even on the field I was
Always in service
So that big ole' open space became my
       Westbury Music Fair, my
       Radio City Music Hall, my
       Naza Coliseum.
Dad's team was
So good that the ball almost
Never came down my side of the field anyway.

Well on this
Brentwood soccer field lesson day,
I saw the crowd cheering.
They were looking at me
And the more I sang,
    the more they cheered
So I kep' on sangin'.
I was singing more
        and more
And then I saw him.
I saw my best friend,
Gray.
Grayson Scarborough was his name.
And he
Used to be on my dad's team.
And he was the other team's forward

And he was coming at me.
But he's my best friend.
He won't let me look bad.
> Gray wouldn't do that to me.
> We share lunch and snacks.
> He's in on my ploy to get extra
> snack twice a week at snack-time.
But he sure is coming fast...
It don't look like that
Soccer ball is slowing down.
"INTERMISSION!"

Sure Gray is fast
And he is talented
But he is my friend,
> my best friend,
> my only friend,
> my first best friend.

He has to have seen me by now.
Gray moves
And maneuvers the ball towards me.
I probably have a decent chance of
Getting the ball away...if do it now.
"It's me, Gray!"

He sees
Me and then,
He does it;
Gray
Kicks the ball past me.

I see the opening to the right of me.
Man, David is wide open and Adrian,
      the other full-back-half-back-goal guardian...
Where is he?

No one else
Makes the same allowances for me.
My first best friend
Didn't.
No one else
Makes the same allowances for me.
My first best friend
Didn't. My last best friend
Didn't.
No one ever
Makes the same allowances
For this Moses.
Now 27, I'm
Still on the soccer field.
Still expecting someone
To make me look good so we
Both can be even.
Not only does man-sized understanding
Say, "right never comes" but "even is non-existent."

No one ever
Makes the same allowances.
No one ever does.
No one ever
Made the same allowances for Moses.
No one ever did.

No one else
Made the same allowances
For *this* Moses.
No one else
Was ever supposed to.

What made
Me Moses not enter in back then?
I made too many allowances;
        too many denials of what was
In me to do
And be
Just so that I could hear
        and be a part of that old familiar hymn,
        "We."
Winning didn't matter
But we-ing was my G.E.T.O.:
        my   Grammy,
                Emmy,
                Tony
                and Oscar.
We-ing will land me straight in the
Haute ghetto too if I
Keep it up too much longer.

No more encores and
No more wecores at the
Sake of a mecore.

Mm.
I guess I really have yet to

Enter beyond the veil
Because I'm
      still and
      still
      always weing,
Trying to wait and make room
For my buddies to enter with me-
      buddy-mama,
      buddy-Sr.,
      buddy-brothers,
      buddy-pillar,
      buddy-raven,
      buddy-wife-to-be,
      buddy-children-to-be—
Just buddies, in general.

Mm.
No mo' mo. No more encores.
The Crowd is tired and this song is played.

A-side on the 45 inch

I know I didn't do anything wrong yesterday but I went to sleep and woke up feeling dirty, feeling prostituted, feeling naïve and without direction. My mind pondered so many "what ifs" concerning how I got home and whether or not or rather, "when" would I have opened my mouth and defended myself. I feel less than although I know I am more than a conqueror. I need a divine revelation to keep me from this feeling that this is what my life has become and in some aspect, will always be.

Dax, big brother, when do I move out of neutral into drive? I've done this reverse thing more than I ever thought I would, but it's this neutral

"HELP!"

existence that keeps me without true identity and sense of self-empowerment. Why am I 27 and I still can't defend myself? Why does my "no" still mean nothing? I'm not 3 or 9 trying to make sense of why these two men are molesting me…it's 24 and 16 years later and I still can't move my mouth to say "stop", to say "no", to say "I don't want this," to say "I'm not playing your games, let me out." Davis, why do I now (and have always) had a willing heart toward God but a mouth that is powerless at articulating my exertion of what I want and don't want?

From the message on the locusts, I now realize I can't blame the man from yesterday or the persons with whom I live or the persons who have moved in and out of the apartment or the politics and choices of the people in my industry and in particular circles. Before I ever met any of them I still had these problems.

One, I've never been able to recognize that my will and physical, emotional or financial well-being were being taken advantage of by male authority figures until it was too late. That's not it. It's that even when I first comprehended the true intent, knew what was going on, and stood up for myself, my voice, my word meant nothing. If it had power, then it would have stopped. It never stopped. It never stops. Two, I have a pattern of risking everything to be available to a male who is brokenhearted by reason of his childhood, home, or sexual abuse. In-House brothers, peers, lawyers, coaches, preachers, singers, promoters, and even once perceived enemies; doesn't matter. That is why I lost Lena. Because I got caught up in a situation that got too complicated and even after it was over, my heart was still not 100% God's much less hers. I don't blame her for walking. I was the fool for expecting her to stay. (She's not Betty Faye or Minnie Jean).

I need help brother. I need help because, not on purpose, but just because of yesterday I feel like I need to get ready for a new round of this mess. It took 2 plus years back home in Jerusalem to really be healed of all that I lost in college because of this heart defect. The yield of my ways was the loss of my self-esteem (that I am a good man), the ability to love anyone, and the ability to feel worthy to receive love from anyone; all of this because I exercised poor judgment and made allowances for certain brothers…in Christ. I need help, bro. The spirit of sexual perversion the molestations imparted to me by those two men is once again trying to become a part of me…and I know it's not. Nevertheless, I find myself losing more of myself at different parts of my life.

Pastor Jenkins preached it, "God raised up the locusts." God did. But the promise is if His people turned back, He would restore what the locusts had taken. I don't want Isaac (my Infiniti) back or Lena, the times in the studio or even my music ministry in Jerusalem; but I <u>do</u> <u>want</u> a <u>restoration</u>. I want the joy of being in a relationship with a woman again and she has my heart. I've had that before; it was wonderful. But now, the ability to consistently exercise wise judgment in *any* area of my life seems impaired.

Through everything that's happened in Babylon, what has boggled my mind the most is the fact that had God given me my own family, had Lena and I gotten married before He opened these doors for run-way modeling or before I walked into a land that didn't require me to be perfect, where I could expose a 20-year-long secret and admit that when I look at my life and my experiences some things just don't fit, I still would have risked it all. Not that God didn't ordain for me to be free, but the liberty to just be… w/o rules or expectations to be good all the time was so foreign to my life's journey that I would have gambled away something real just to have one chance at momentary wings.

Man, this is so not about what I should have done or said to ward off this guy's unwanted advances. It's not about a date, sex, attraction, flirtation or stealing a nigger is his chest so he gets the message. Had I stole him, it would have been a one time act; not a change in the lexicon or paradigms of my life. What I need is boldness in my spirit and Divine liberty in my mind so that I will never again make choices or non-choices that jeopardize me. That is my prayer request—that the boldness and liberty that come with the Holy Spirit would come forth in me, now. You know I feel handicapped because I don't have the stature of my father and most of my brothers, (6'3", 6'4", 6'8" and all a solid 225), so I gotta rest on the Spirit of God to bring forth these things in the spirit of Moses.

I know you've gotten a lot today; but my feeling this way, like I've done something wrong because I just sat there and didn't defend or stand up for my self, is the enemy's condemnation. But, it's this same very feeling that can make you feel unworthy of being part of the Body or (for me) of even wanting to be around people.

And isolation always leads to deeper sin.

This is my record of help.

gracechild's note: the following short story was one of several stories I wrote years ago as a graduation requirement from Syracuse University. It was originally entitled, "I Shall Not Be Moved." It was renamed because I came to a point of personal understanding of childhood, not particularly mine, but of what childhood is supposed to do in preparing you for your calling. "Stood On The Banks Of Jordan" is dedicated to that which has come since first writing this piece and that which is yet to come in my relationship with my father, Moses Thomas [Alexander] Greene, Sr. Hey dad, "We've come a long way, baby." Mo.

I found it very difficult to go back and "perfect" this work while in exile. I believe it is the most powerful, telling work of my pre-exile. During this phase of my life I was at the point of accusing; now I am in the state of becoming. I am no longer, in my heart, in this place of turmoil. So much has been dealt with and I have received so many answers to so many questions that were camouflaged in the language in this text.

So the question remains, Why include it in "my proposal: nothing but a gracechild: the revelations of a prodigal son now in GOD-caused exile"? I have chosen to include it because this story was my way of crying out to be heard all those years ago. This story was my father's Christmas gift of December 1994. It was my way of saying, "Dad, I have a whole lot of unsettled parts of me." As a searcher for the truth of who I am in Christ and in and as a part my dad, what I discovered was too powerful for Bay Shore, my familiar world, my Jerusalem and the ministry to which I belonged. My wonderful time of revelation in the year 2000 has come because of what I sowed back then. I am experiencing this level of freedom because six years ago I purposed to confront, uncover and deal with every imbalance of my existence; even if that was due to my perception alone.

You may be crying for help or a family member may be crying for help. Crying for answers to some of the whys of their being. It may not be in a form that is familiar enough to you. Slow down, take notice of your environment. God may still have you at home or may have stilled you to return back home not because you didn't make the right choices along the way or because you were not led by the Holy Spirit in the decisions you made. Perhaps God is giving you the chance to "stand on the banks of Jordan." My Jordan River was a man named Moses, my father. I got it now. I didn't find me until I understood that my dad was scheduled to be me, a man (some call intellectual in nature) with the love of language, learning, education and the communications industry, in theatre and a proclaimer of the Gospel...but life interrupted, and left him bereft. Life interrupts us all but it doesn't always leave us bereft. Maybe your father, your mother, your uncle or that authority figure in your life is how they are or was how they were and became what they became because life interrupted, and left them bereft.

For some, a war may have interrupted where you saw your life going. For others, an unplanned pregnancy, the premature death of a parent or the divorce of your parents. In my life, my first step in fully being reconciled with my dad was to honor the grace on his life to have survived. Because of God's grace, the person dear to your heart has survived as well. However, for us who are in the shadows of another's overflow, it remains a gift from God that we would receive the opportunity to stand on the banks of their experiences.

The ministry opportunity divinely appointed to you is to fulfill Isaiah 61. Let the Spirit of the Lord come upon you, nu'ahch (rest upon) you and anoint you to preach good tidings to the poor, to gather the broken pieces of those persons' hearts and heal them; to proclaim liberty to those who are still captive by life's interruption(s) and to command the opening of the prison to those bound.

Yeah, this story marks John's crying out in the wilderness. As you read, I invite you to get understanding; then heal yourself. As you heal, then heal those closest and furthest from you in the understanding that you are where you are and are who you are-still standing- not because of any series of things you controlled, but because of God's amazing grace.

From the Greene House, Moses Thomas Alexander
June 24, 2000 3:34 PM
Minor additions March 14, 2001 4:24 PM
Final addition October 5, 2001 12:24 PM

Stood On The Banks Of Jordan...

I shall not, I shall not be moved.
I shall not, I shall not be moved.
Just like a tree planted by the waters
I shall not be moved.

Is it possible for a tree to be planted so close to the waters and it never take root? This is how Pha-raoh felt. He seemed consumed by the tides although he lived amongst trees. For Pha-raoh, no rivers ever ran through his desert nor were there any ways that led out of his wilderness.

He lived not knowing; feeling but never truly knowing. His life's questions could never be answered with a simple "yes" or "no." This created within him a mindset of uncertainty. The uncertainty begat complacency. Complacency begat resentment; resentment, rejection; rejection, apathy and when apathy completed its perfect work, that which was never supposed to occur because of Whose child Pha-raoh was, did. Hatred, undeniably the most-complete and perfected mutant of Love was brought forth and it "spored" daily out of his heart.

From the essence of his inner man, Pha-raoh felt that the hatred which had not yet seized his soul was just metamorphosed, backslidden Love. He spent most of his life fighting to reclaim the pure Love that had been napped from him. He knew that it could only come from the One who was greater than the hate *himself*.

The Lord would use his life as a song for others like him who had felt rejected by every thing male, every thing that they aspired to be but failed. From his experience would flow lyrics. His tears would be the dynamite needed to sing with conviction and through his triumphs he would be given a story to share with others. This is the story *behind* the story that enabled Pha-raoh Cedric Banks to draw many to Christ. This is Pha-raoh's story. This is Pha-raoh's song.

GENESIS 1:1-2
In the beginning God created the heaven and the earth.
And the earth was without form and void...

They were brothers. "Is it possible for a tree to be planted so close to the waters and it never take root?" Blood. The greatest distance between Pha-raoh and his younger brother Niles was the four-and-a-half feet between their bedroom doors, yet it seemed as if each lived with an innate hatred for the other...now. Ever-striving to be pleasing in God's sight, even at this young age Pha-raoh searched within himself *first* to find the source. What could have produced it? Could the answer lie solely in Niles' height? Know. Not only was Niles taller but also lighter and stronger than the ashy, dusty brown Pha-raoh. This had been the case since they were five and seven years old so he dared not look at any of those things as the sperm and egg of the loathsome spirit that grew inside him.

Pha-raoh had never been tall like their father but occupied an average height like their mother and her side of the family. In a family where every man is at least six-four, light-skinned, with a high-butt, long, naturally built legs and muscle-bound arms, (the latter two for all the balls a man needed to be a man), where did Pharaoh fit in? The truth, Pha-raoh's heart-felt truth, was that he didn't fit in. In height, he was average and in strength he was average and in complexion he was the average black, little boy. In school he wasn't allowed to be average so he wondered why God would allow him to have an average existence. To be average included being everything that being exceptional, that being great and tremendous didn't. Pha-raoh would never be tall like their father but would occupy an average height like his mother and her side of the family.

He was close to her, Isha Phaye. As long as she was there Pha-raoh could bear all of the nots in his life. He felt spiritually and physically linked to her in ways that went deeper than the umbilical. He never had this same sense of belonging in his relationship with his father.

Although there was no doubt that Jordan Banks was the father...blood...of both he and Niles, each day stirred within Pha-raoh a feeling of he having been adopted. This is how it had always been. There was never a time when he felt that he was truly a part of Jordan; at least not as much as he knew Niles was. Pha-raoh <u>was</u> moved and would always be because he felt half planted. How would this tree bear fruit without the answer every man-child searched for: the why to his existence and to his father's lack of love.

MARK 4:17
*"And have not root in themselves,
and so endure but for a time...*

Pha-raoh was sown deeper onto stony ground every time he went shopping with Isha Phaye. It never failed. *It never failed.* Whether they were in Pathmark or Modell's down on First and Adams Boulevard, the sisters from New Jerusalem or Allen A.M.E. Zion, (where his grandmother belonged), would come up to them and say, "Isha Phaye, how you gurl?" Not really asking a question or seeking an answer because through the many years of their acquaintance with her they knew that her response would always be, "I'm blessed." Then they would address Pha-roah; he was always their second thought. "Li'l Pha-raoh, you look more and more like your mama e'vryday." They would lean into Isha Phaye, whisper loud enough for any one in aisle twelve to hear, "You sho' Jor'n his dadae?" and then offer up such cackling that it drew others' attention to them. "He ain't got no Banks on him." Then they'd bend down and say, "You're a Nun if I ever saw one. Swear you look just like yo' mama's brothers Jesse and.. .uh.. .uhm. . .what's the real dark one's name...," someone would start, "Col-" "Colonel Lee, that's right, ah-hunh."

Now at any time did they think about what they were saying? Not really a question. The entire exchange reinforced within Pha-raoh the feeling that he got nothing from his father.

"Bless God, you got Isha Phaye's moles, smile and eyelashes. You yo' mama's chile!"
Not only did these three things further distance Pha-raoh from

Jordan and Niles, (without their having acted in any way), but they sounded like a nursery-rhyme-formula to create orphans. "Moles, smile and eyelashes." (Pha-raoh's definition of orphans: (oar-fins) n. Children born not knowing.)

Eyelashes. How functional a creation! They were to protect the eye from dirt, dust, debris and the like. Eyelashes. Eyelashes. Isha Phaye's were fake, Pha-raoh's were real. This was all right because to Pha-raoh they were the only things not real on his mother. Eyelashes. Eyelashes. Eyelash. His father's were most definitely real...and long.

COLOSSIANS 3:20
"Children, obey your parents in all things:
for this is well pleasing unto the Lord."

What type of fruit would a tree planted on good ground but xylemed with rejection and phloemed with disobedience produce? Not really a question.

His father...well....Pha-raoh despised him and it *seemingly* went both ways. His mother always said to him, "You've got to remember that your daddy didn't have a father..." and would go on and on and on. That was supposed to be the reason why he didn't know how to express his love for Pha-raoh. But if that was the case, why could he show Niles love? A question; still, a question.

PSALM 23
"The Lord is my Shepherd..."

Pha-raoh wanted. His pastures were never fully green as the world believed. His reality showed him he had no true pastures, not one blade of green grass...not one, no not one, none. The waters of his life had never been still enough to be led beside; not half the time anyway.

The world believed that Jordan's love for his boys was equal and inexhaustible; that he would do anything for Pha-roah and Niles. But how "the world" needed to be moved. The world didn't have to live in the house, just praise it from outside. Pha-raoh felt that Jordan was behind Niles, and always had been. No one had let the world know, and Pharaoh had not yet reached the age when he could proclaim, that after love hammered in the last nail of the house that she had built, she kept gettin' up. Love got in the wind baby! One woe for the world, another for the sad, lost souls who dwell in the house. Still one woe remains.

The house of division was set. It was this life of feeling alienated by father, loved by mother, rejected as caregiver by brother that shaped his childhood. Dinnertime was especially hard for Pha-raoh. Nightly he sat in between criticism and rejection and across from his mother. Every time he looked up he saw everything that he wanted to be, but make it male.

One Tuesday night he decided that he wasn't going to take it any more. If Jordan hit him across the knuckles with the sharp side of the knife he would ask him, "What's the matter fool!" Well he wouldn't say "fool" because his Sunday School lesson taught him that he shouldn't say it, but he would say something. "Jerk" would get him backslapped, but for that matter so would "fool." He came to a conclusion. He would say, "dad," but with an attitude.

He was joking and his father warned him to stop. He did. Niles started telling jokes and was warned to stop but kept on.

"Dad, you're not going to say anything?"

Pha-raoh waited for the knife but who was he kidding. Niles would never get hit.

"Daddy, ain' shtupid," Niles said. Everyone looked up. "He know better than to hit my hands," Niles continued. Now that dare didn't deserve a shaking? A grabbing at the collar? A clenching of the forearm?

Pha-raoh looked left at Jordan. Nothing. To Niles and then to the air for the motion of the knife towards Niles' hands. Nothing. To Isha Phaye, she bit her lip and looked down. Nothing. He looked bewildered, dismayed. "Be not dismayed whatever beniled. " He couldn't hide it. He had to be dismayed...or maybe not. If Niles didn't get it for what he said, what could Pha-raoh possibly say that would make Jordan hit him?

Minutes later, Pha-raoh had been telling jokes for minutes and had already gotten one stern, "Watch yourself, boy" from Jordan. In the back, front and hind parts of his mind he was being fueled by, "If Niles didn't get it for telling Daddy *to his face* that he knows better then to hit his hands," I'm gonna keep on going. And once

Pha-raoh got going, stories would just be rolling off his tongue. You knew he was lying when he would announce, "And I'm not telling stories."

"...So...so...so, and I'm not telling stories, today in gym class, Cynthia went up to A.J. and said, 'A.J.', and I'm not telling stories, 'if your mother ain't...ain't got no legs why they choose her to lead that song, 'Step To Jesus'?" Niles would be falling out of his chair, Isha Phaye would be laughing and Jordan would just be eating.

"And...and...and...and then A.J. went up to Cynthia with her big bug eye and said, and I'm not telling stories, 'Well yo mama ain't got no arms or no hands and they let her sing, 'Lift Him Up'. "

By now, Niles would be on the floor kicking the ground, Isha would be leaned backward wiping tears from her eyes, and Jordan...just eating.

"And then, and then, and I'm not telling stories, and then *I* said, 'Na-unhh, A.J., na-unhh. If her mom had arms and legs, she wooddint need to sing that special part.'"

"What special part?" asked Niles.

"Somebody hep me, -Hep me liff Jesus."

"CaPOWWW!" came the knife in one fierce, plundering prick.

"I said, 'Quit playing around!'" screamed his father. Before he could say what he had practiced all afternoon in his mirror, his nose started quivering with a strong sensation, his throat got a sharp, almost throbbing pain and he started sniffling all over his food. Then... tears came.

He looked to his mother, then to Niles and lastly, his father. Isha Phaye looked back at him and brought her lips together in an effort to restrain her tongue. He knew that she was being there for him. Niles looked at him and then without reservation said, "Daddy, can I have another piece of steak?" Pha-raoh balled. The night's dinner served as another occasion where Niles would get the well done that Pha-raoh felt he would never have.

"Stop crying and finish your dinner," his mother said.

Pha-raoh stuffed his mashed potatoes and country peas in his mouth. He tried the steak, but it was too tough for his teeth. Clear, cry snut flowed to the tip of his lip.

"May I be excused?" he asked.

"Wipe your face, son" his mother returned.

He did.

"May I be excused?" he asked again.

"You better stop crying 'fore I *give* you something to cry

about. You want that?"

"No," Pharaoh solemnly returned.

"Speak up. YOU WANT THAT!"

Jordan had reached his unbearable level of anger that Isha Phaye just could not handle.

"Come on Jordan."

"I'm talking to Pha-raoh right now Isha, all right!"

Now they would get into it and it wouldn't end until the wee hours of the morning.

"No, you're badgering the poor kid. He was just telling a joke Jordan, just a joke. God, can't any one laugh in this house?"

"It's all right mommy."

Isha Phaye, by now disgusted, got up from the table and went upstairs to their bedroom.

"Finish your food Ph...."

Jordan looked down and unexpectedly saw all of his food gone. "Go on upstairs and finish your homework."

"Can I watch Family Feud?"

"What time does it come on?"

"7 30."

"Mmm. If all of your homework is done."

Pha-raoh got up and walked out of the kitchen. As he hit the first step leading upstairs, to his refuge from the wildlife (his room), he heard Niles ask, "Can I go over Jamie' s?"

"Is all your homework finished?"

"Yes."

He knew that Niles' homework wasn't done. *Everyone* knew that Niles' homework was not done. It was the tradition of Niles, which he exercised at least four out of five of the school nights, to come in at 7:30 right before bath time and remember that he had one worksheet on times tables or something.

But that was life and he had to deal with it. Now he didn't want to seem ungrateful because he was told God had been too good for him to complain. He knew that somewhere there existed children who were less "forchanet" than he was, but he didn't care about all of that. He desired goodness from his father down here. Sure, Jordan was a hardworking man, but if all that work made him yell and treat him and his mother like dirt, he figured that he would rather his father not work or not come home, one.

No one was allowed to close the doors to their rooms at any time, but once in his room, he closed *his* door and cried on his bed. The pillow heard all of that day's sorrows and felt a river of grief. Isha Phaye came in the room and sat beside him.

"Come on, come on baby...shhh, shhh. Listen," she wiped his face with her hand; tears, snot and all, "you didn't do nothing wrong, you hear me?"

"I.. I. I. .j.j.just was trying to have s. .ss.ssssome fun mommy. He didn't smack Niles an...an and stupid Niles even dared him to."

Isha Phaye pressed her baby to her chest and just rocked him.

"I know baby. You gotta remember that at your father's house they weren't allowed to talk..."

She always would try to get Pha-raoh to understand that his father, because of so many nots in his life, didn't know how to show love. They talked for another couple of minutes and then Pha-raoh, really a comedian at heart, would make Isha Phaye laugh by saying something like,

"When I grow up and he comes to my house, every time he opens his mouth, 'BAMM!' I'm gonna hit his knuckles. He's gonna ask for a napkin...BAMM!; some ice for his tea, "BAMM!" a fork...'BAMM!' I'm gonna be like Aunt Essie down South with a fly swatter for her roaches. And just like Aunt Essie can look right dead at you and see the roach running from behind her toaster and swat him and not miss a beat, he gonna be talking about, "Yeah man, I was driving down on ninety-five and got all the way to" – "caPowwAMM! "Shut up."

By this time, the two of them would be cracking up. The door would open.

"Who closed this door?"

"I did," answered Isha Phaye.

"What's the matter with him?"

"Nothing Jordan, he just wanted to talk."

Jordan would walk down to their bedroom and Pha-raoh would react but now playfully. "What's the matter? Man tried to cut off my hands and he wants to know what's the matter."

"Get your work done, son"

She would hug him, kiss him and then say, "I love you."

"I love you too mommy."

Before he would work he would have to get some sleep. He was always sleepy after his father made him cry. Pha-raoh walked over to the phonograph that his grandfather gave him. He took out his favorite record; the one with a white cover and the black pencil drawing of James Cleveland that everybody had. He put it on song three. He just liked the words of the song.

First came the sounds, echoes of people. Even then Pha-raoh could see them packed tight is some hot church. James' voice would saunter in, "I stood on the banks of Jurden one day..." and this scratchy sounding ensemble would attack, "to SEE THE SHPS go SAIL LEENG O ver whoooo." But on one chorus Pha-raoh heard this sandpaper tenor belt "Yeahhhhh" and then some woman, a true soprano no doubt, would cover his tenor with a scissoring, "Yaaaaahhhh" that turned into a symphony of power. But this evening, when James got to the second verse, "Lord, you took my mother..." God intervened. God intervened.

Although only nine years old, as Pha-raoh slept, the Lord allowed him to spiritually stand on the banks of his father. He saw everything that his father had been through in life. He saw ships of love, trust and determination leaving the shore only to return with cargo after cargo of disappointments and letdowns. The Lord even unloaded one ship and laid its "treasures" on the banks of Pha-raoh. Pha-raoh became burdened down. The Lord allowed him to feel his father's pain. He stood on Jordan's banks and it hurt and he began to cry. He became angry and wanted to lash out at every one and then, in a small, soft, almost-still voice, the Lord spoke to him.

"Pha-raoh, son...be strong, for the victory ahead will be worth your present problems. Pray for your father. He needs it. Pray now for your mother, she needs it. And pray for Niles. He needs prayer and he needs you. Don't look to your father to be rooted. Look unto me my son. You shall not be moved because you are the tree that it planted by the water. It is not who planted you but because of Whose plant you are. I will not suffer you to be moved."

When he woke up, the record was skipping. "To see the ships, to see the ships, to see the ships."

That next night, Pha-raoh went with Isha Phaye to Wednesday

night service. For hours he sat and watched the sisters, big and yella', thick and chocolate; bony, red-Georgia-clay brown and thin-lipped; red-boned and wide-nosed; shoe-shine-luster-black and straight-, wavy-, curly- or tight-haired, white, wigged or afroed, praise de Lord. All dressed in white, (some of them tastefully, others accessorized with make-shift not real white, beige and even peach belts which snugly fit right beneath their "chest"). They would call out, "Preachit, pastuh!" as Rev. Dr. John B. LaPuta from Louisiana's Cajun country preached on "Goo'ness an' Mersay!"

As the Rev. Dr. preached, Pha-raoh wondered two things: where did he find the time to preach, visit the sick and shut-in *and* make nightly visits to Ms. Bonnie next door with her "condition," (that's how Isha Phaye described it to him). And two, how come when he looked, goodness and mercy were nowhere to be found? Guess they were two strokes behind love!

There would always come a time when, as the Rev. Dr. preached, the church organist, Willie Pearl, would jump on that Hammond, pounce on them keys, beat her left foot on them brown, wooden foot pedals and bless God, she'd have it humming, baby! Then the choir director Ervin would be touched, "whoa!" and start the dance. Ervin and the Rev. Dr. were the only men who danced. Pha-raoh wanted to be like them. Ervin moved fast like a little Peter Cottontail on the run from Isha Phaye for messing in her garden. Pha-raoh believed that the Holy Ghost was in Ervin's hair because wherever that Jeri curl juice flew, someone would be touched with the dance. In no time that juice was everywhere! Erv, all of the women-especially Isha Phaye, and the Rev. Dr.

would be shoutin', smacking each other and falling out for at least an hour.

"Sing a new song unto the Lord..."

There was always a song on his lips. Jordan and Niles hated going places with he and Isha Phaye because they always sang. In the car they sang, as they watched TV they sang, even their words in regular conversation seemed to have melodic tones behind them. Isha Phaye always encouraged Pha-raoh to let his song out, in spite of what *people* said. She once told him of a "time times time and a half" ago when the gift of song had been beaten out of her. She told him that it was in those moments when she knew that she had received a gift. "Baby, if I could sing while I was being thrown around by the storm-tossed seas of life," she laughed, "and love," she stroked his cheek, "truly God had entrusted me with something special. Every song that you've ever heard me sing, I've already given it back to Him."

Isha Phaye and Pha-raoh sang with their lips but Pha-raoh felt that his entire family sang an ever-changing song. (He felt that he almost *knew* this). There was one tune for the home, another for the church and completely different ones for Parent-Teacher Conference nights and for the ladies at the hot dog truck. Jordan faithfully took he and Niles to the truck on Saturdays after they came back from swimming lessons at the Y.M.C.A. It was in the Y. that he realized he had been entrusted with a similar gift as Isha Phaye.

Pha-raoh was never taught how to swim. He sat on the side

singing for the instructors for eight-weeks while the children his age were swimming. On the last day, when the parents came to see the progress of their children, the poor boy *nearly* drowned. On this day, he would not only face but overcome the life-threatening waters. Upon setting foot on Canaan's shore, Pha-raoh vowed to himself and to his Father that he would never again allow the rough waters of Egypt to toss him neither to nor fro.

EXODUS 14:21

"And Moses stretched out his hand over the sea;
and the Lord caused the sea to go back."

The time came for the little boys and girls to show what strokes they had learned. Everyone was doing well. Pha-raoh's turn came...and went. He succeeded in talking his way out of going when the "B's" came up. Joey Zimmerman had just finished a graceful swim. It was as if his body was made for the water. The instructors and parents cheered him on but Ethel, his mother, had to order him out of the water because after a while "he started showing his behind." The eleven to twelve-year-old's were ready to go next and so Pha-raoh had to go. "Pha-raoh Banks! Come on son, it's your turn!" Pha-raoh looked up.

"Just like a tree planted by the waters..."

Pha-raoh trusted God. He walked to the diving board and like every kid that went up there, made sure his parents were looking. He walked to the edge of the board and got his first good look at the water. He saw his reflection in the water. Fear came but before he knew it, mother Henry's favorite hymn, "Take Me To The

Water," escaped from his soul and through his lips.

Lord knows how that woman loves that song! One time the membership had gathered at the church because Hurricane Helen was tearing apart all of Long Island. The church was filled with, not only members but, those men and women, "the ain'ts." See the saints come regularly, but the ain'ts...well, well...you only see twice a year on Mother's Day and on Easter Sunday. Anyway, short, stout and overly sweet Deac' Jones prayed a good-little-ole prayer, anointed and all. Everybody was up in a praise, *especially* the ain'ts. Jones then asked for the saints, ain'ts, utmost and guttermost to allow for the flow of the Holy Spirit and to let the Spirit give them a song. Everybody knew that what he really wanted was an upbeat praise song that would encourage every one's spirit and get their minds off the storm and onto the Sonshine.

With all of that rain being thrown down from heaven's faucet and the fierce winds knocking over cars, houses and some churches and the flooding going on, what did mother Henry belt out? That's right, "Take Me To The Water!" If she would have seen the gazes of all who sat behind her, Mother Henry would have died right on the spot. Some people started laughing the small "smnh-smnh" laughs they usually make more noise than just laughing out loud. To break the tension, Jordan made the entire church laugh because just as Mother Henry broke out into the second line, he screamed in a country bumpkin tone , "Alls yuh gotta do is go outside!"

PSALM 113:3A

"From the rising of the sun...

Back to the Y. Time had passed and by now Pha-raoh, (according to the song), had been baptized three times and still had not jumped into the waters. The entire scene was unbelievable. That little boy of seventy-eight pounds had the crowd humming softly and tenderly as he gave a mini-sermonette on why he wasn't scared to jump into the waters. He said, "If I want to, I can walk on it." Whether he walked on it, skipped, ran, did back flips or sank in it, Black and white folk alike just wanted him off the board so they could see their children and go home. *This* day wasn't God's day for him to walk *on* the water, but he would have to stretch out and go *through* the water.

PSALM 113:3B

..... until the going down of the same..."

Parents had grown tired and were now willing to do just about anything to get him to jump. Pha-raoh had the crowd at his feet. The bony boy even got Vinny's father, Rabbi Goldschwitz, to belt out three choruses of "I love Jesus, yes I do!"

Pha-raoh finished the song. His mother clapped as tears streamed down her face. Niles joined in after he recovered from laughter (which had led him to the floor). Jordan looked at him blankly. Amazed.

Pha-raoh looked into the water and then jumped up and down on the board. He heard, "You can do it son!" then saw his mother stand up. He jumped up again and again, again and again, again-again, again.. .whew! ... again.. .he looked at the crowd, smiled and waved, they smiled and waved back at him.. .he jumped again-again and now higher.

> *"Time is winding up, time is winding up,*
> *Time is winding up, Oh-oh time is winding up."*

Pha-raoh had now been jumping, just straight up and down, for exactly two minutes and thirty three seconds, but no one dared to move him.

LUKE 21:8

"...and the time draweth near..."

By the fourth minute, the children were irate and several parents had approached Jah Arnold, the instructor.

LUKE 21:19

"In your patience possess ye your souls."

Five minutes down.

LUKE 21:28A

"And when these things begin to come to pass...

Pha-raoh continued to jump.

LUKE 21:28 B

...Then look up, and lift up your heads;

for your redemption draweth nigh."

He stopped suddenly, looked out over the water, his eyes being transfixed on something and then broke out into "I Shall Not Be Moved." The line of kids behind him started screaming, "Jump Pha-raoh, Jump!" but Pha-raoh kep' on singing. All the parents except two threatened to withhold their fees for the day if Jah didn't make Pha-raoh jump. Pharaoh kep' on singing. He got as far as, "Just like a tree planted by the-" when Ju-Ju Lucasen scurried up the steps to the board, ran behind him and pushed Pha-raoh off.

A surprised Pha-raoh, whose eyes were still stuck on the waters, continued to sing from the top of his lungs as his body awkwardly jerked forward. Jordan ran to the waters edge. Still singing, somehow Pharaoh's body changed mid-air and his back slammed against the water. Still singing, Pha-raoh's feet followed his back.

REVELATIONS 20:6
"IT IS DONE..."

Isha Phaye ran to the edge, Niles followed. Pha-raoh sank toward the bottom of the over fifteen feet deep pool as all of the parents ran to the waters edge. Jordan called out to him but Pha-raoh's rigid body continued sinking like a lifeless rock. As his body sank, his voice somehow continued to be heard. He didn't kick one foot, stroke an arm or even move his head but somehow Pha-raoh was still singing that song.

Caught. Before Pha-raoh's body reached the bottom of the pool, "something" caught him. He opened his eyes and saw a Light brighter than he had ever seen before surrounding him. Although it was just light, Pha-raoh felt comforted and more at peace than he had ever felt in his life. A hand reached out from the light and touched through his Adam's apple to his vocal chords.

"Pha-raoh!" his fathers called; one anxiously, the other calmly. A voice from the light instructed him, "Sing my son, sing. Use this gift to face all of the waters in your life."

"Swim Pha-raoh!" his brothers encouraged; one nervously, the other patiently. Blood was thicker than water.

"I don't know how to swim."

The light faded, but Pha-raoh didn't want it to leave. "No!"

The voice said, "Use the power that I have given you. Put your back to the waters son. It's all behind you."

Pha-raoh was starting to float to the top.

"Come on here Pha-raoh!" screamed Isha Phaye.

He didn't want to the leave the light but knew that he had power of the waters. A song rang from his newly delivered soul,

"Gonna lay down my troubles, down by the riverside."

"That's it," encouraged the voice. "Down by the riverside."

"Come on Pha-raoh," encouraged his brother. "Down by the riverside..."

The hand touched Pha-raoh's foot and with great power, his body shot out of the waters and about three feet into the air above the waters. This time when his back hit the waters on its way down, it glided on the waters' surface. Jah and every one stood around amazed.

"Lord, have mercy," said Jordan. Slowly Pha-raoh began doing the backstroke.

"Pha-raoh?" questioned his brother.

This had to be impossible. The eight to ten year old's weren't taught the backstroke, so how could he...?

Not only was he swimming, but still singing. "Tell me how didja' feel when you, come out the wilderness." He sang and swam this tune for ten minutes. Then he broke out into the extended version of his second father's favorite song, "I shall not be moved."

The voice that came from his little body was so strong and so anointed that he made the song his own.

Pha-raoh swam and sang for thirteen minutes when suddenly, half way across the pool his stroking stopped... his head sank and...a "Jesus!" was heard. He was drowning.

"Jesus! Jesus!...whoolup...Jesus!" Jah and the other the instructors ran along side the pools edge and jumped in when they got close enough to his body. Too late, Isha Phaye had already leaped in; wool pants, homemade blouse, gold wedding band and all. She was too late too. Jordan had already reached his firstborn.

Jordan lifted his son out of the water and Pha-raoh screamed,

> "Thank you Jesus, you saved me! You picked me up and brought me out of the waters!" He thrashed around so much that Jordan couldn't hold him alone.

> "Jesus! Jesus! Jesus!" Pha-raoh continued screaming.

Isha Phaye reached her husband and their first son. "No, it's mommy and daddy. Just stand up boy," she said.

> "Jesus! Thank you for bringing me through!" he continued.

> "The water's not deep. Stand up!" added Jordan.

Coughing, but praising God, Pharaoh stood up. He grabbed his father and said,

> "Daddy you don't understand, before I hit the bottom of the pool, I was caught by... Daddy listen to me, Jesus!"

No one understood. Isha Phaye looked to Jordan as they guided their son out of the waters.

Niles, seeing that Pharaoh was all right, ran back toward the swimmers, found Ju-Ju and just started smackin' that boy around. With each word Ju-Ju got a slap: "I-told-you-that-no-one-was-to-move-my-brother! Didn't I!" Somehow Niles smack the boy six times on "didn't I."

They stood Pha-raoh up on the bleachers. Jordan reached out his hand and pulled him to his chest. "You awright boy?"

Silence. Could Jordan really care? Know.

"I swam daddy."
"Yes, son. You swam."

Niles. Niles? Chris Tyson's grandmother, Mother Mare, rescued "Juice-Juice," as she called him, from Niles but now she was whipping Niles. She later told Isha Phaye and Jordan that Niles disrespected her when she told him to stop hitting Juice-Juice and he kept on going.

That night, when the going-ons of the day were finally over and he had the chance to reflect upon all that had happened, he laid in his bed and cried silently; like he had done so many nights before. But on this night, he cried for a different reason.

"Saints, before I sing my last song of the evening, there is a special surprise that I have for someone in the audience. That someone is my father, Jordan Banks...stand up dad.

"Yes, yes...it was in those waters of the Y. that I found Jesus. He gave me a mandate to use the gift of song, as a way not only to magnify Him but to use it as a ministry for fathers and for sons everywhere. I sing this next song for all of the fathers, but especially for my dad.

Pha-raoh looked through his father's eyes into their past together. He sojourned, "I stood on the banks of Jordan, one day, just to..."

"To see the ships go sailing over..." rang gently from His back up singers, Niles and Junari, better known as Ju-Ju. And with every ounce of forgiveness that Pha-raoh had been given he gave it back to his father in this next verse.

"The Lord allowed me to stand on the banks of Jordan, I had to see the ships go by."

As Pha-raoh left the stage and walked into the audience the back up singers repeated, "to see the ships." He reached his father and they embraced. The audience stood to their feet and worshipped the Lord. Father and son worshipped the Lord. Brother and brother worshipped the Lord. With his father by his side, Pha-raoh ended the song,

"I had to see the ships go-o-o by."

Pha-raoh held on to that last note as he had held on to God's word these many years. The longer he held the note, the sweeter it became and the more convicting it became. Yokes of bondage were broken all over the building.

Pha-raoh went back to the stage. It took all Jordan had to keep himself together. He tried to grip Isha Phaye's hand but that wasn't enough. Tears ran down his face as he rocked back and forth.

GENESIS 1:2B

"And the spirit of God moved upon the face of the waters"

Jordan was free and now knew that blood was thicker than the waters.

The instruments continued to play as fathers and sons all over the audience embraced. Men who had wrestled with the spirits of homosexuality, violation, abandonment, bi-sexuality, negative self-identity and rejection because they didn't feel loved enough by their fathers now prayed about their souls' states. Many embraced the Blood, for they too finally knew it was thicker than the waters.

In that one song, Hallelujah, the hatred, gone; the feelings of neglect, gone; the resentment of over twenty years; gone; not just gone but cast into the sea of Manasseh. Just like the Tree of Life planted by the Fountains of Living Waters, Pha-raoh no longer hungered, neither did he thirst and most assuredly, most blessedly, he was not moved.

electric company
(abridged version)

123456789101112
123456789101112
ABCDEFGHIJKLMNOPQRSTUVW

X

Too much to lose. **Too much**
at stake. **Too** **much** for it not
to be real. **Too much** for it not
to be
consistent.

If it was to be
it would have been.

Heck, we've had
time
and
if there really was
(in our heart's heart)
an "it" for us to be,
we would have crossed that finish line.

Too much for it
to, at times,
be a game.

Too much for there
to be
days of semantics.

I told myself a while back that I didn't have time to walk with
anyone who spoke semantics when it came to my destiny. Most of
our communication, that which *arouses*, is not even a play on
words; it's semantics.

Still afraid to ask where
and with whom you've been
since the last time.

Even more afraid for myself
as my heart doesn't believe the answers even when I
hear them.

I want a love that isn't scared to ask any questions and ready to hear answers.

This isn't it
as
there
is   still **too much**
iffy communication.

I have a love,   but
I want   to live
the love.

Too much   for us
to stay   like this.

We   can't
even walk together   because
we both have
individual
days of agreement
and disagreement
of who we are   and want to be to the other.

What is our significance?
How are we defined—to us alone?
...

Love

has never

been

a

question;

at least not for me. But holiness, its display and carriage, by **both** of us, has left much to be desired...by God.

So before
    I hurt unto death,
        long into sickness,
        become ravished by a bankrupted destiny
or

    infiltrate hell's walls,

I	give you	up.
I	give you	over.
I		**now trust God**
alone		**because**
I	**have learned** that	with
	the right set of	gray situations,
		I
		can't
		even
		trust
		my
		own
		heart.

This isn't a game; it's my life.
Not that any of the games played,
        semantics-spoken,
        words miscommunicated
were done on
        or
        off purpose,
it's just that life happened...
to both of us.

No   doomsday prayer,
no   expectation for you
to completely disappear out of life;
just out of this portion of my heart.

It will
be hard

but in time,

it will
be.

For me, if nothing else, I have gained the strength of my song,
                    the power behind my musical-
                    "If it had not been for the LORD who
                    was on my side..."

I have something,   an experience full of the Master's mercy
                    and goodness
                    and forgiveness
                    and abundant grace

of which now I can sing
                    and play
                    and act
                    and through which I can write,
                    produce, and live a delivered life.

I don't scorn you
but love you all the more.
I don't scorn anything
we have been through
but give
GOD praise because
at least He Chose me for you
and you for me

to go through
this level of warfare.
It could have been
a whole lot worse.
Without God's grace
it would have been
a whole lot worse.

I am confident
of this very thing
that the God
who hath begun a good work in
both of us
is still faithful
to perform it
until the day
of Jesus Christ.

So now,
I'm on to "Y"
and all that comes after
my "X" experience.
Or perhaps,
back to a pre-A existence
of who God wanted me to be...
before I even knew me.

I love you
and
wait
patiently
for all the glory
that will come into,
        out of
        and through
        your life after this,
        your M-experience.

See ya round friend.

M

5:10 pm

The things that die,
in time,
give you the greatest treasure when it comes to your journey.
They are the benchmarks of your growth.
You never can go back.
And even if you try, it—the person, the act, the sensation, the rush,
the mental foreplay, the scheming and all you have to do to get your
it—is not the same. Because you have wrestled with Jesus and
He touched the hollow of your heart's thigh such that it limps,
the true joy of it is gone.
You feel an emptiness, a depth of void that no one, no thing and no
experience can fill.
Some may want a pray-per-view rematch. As for me, I found home.
My power was in finding home.
"Go home" (and then leave it the right way).

when mae
started for home

CHAPTER 7

<u>Prolog: Epi !</u>

It's gonna be early, early in the morning
It's gonna be early, early in the morning
It's gonna be early, early in the morning
Just when i get start for home

Post Independence Day 1999
3:31 AM

My life is forever changed. Great Aunt Mae is dead, she died of a heart attack, of a massive heart attack early this morning. It is affecting me. Oddly enough it's like calling me to a new level in Christ. I have an odd desire to live and to plead to God for my life. Great Aunt Mae's sudden death makes the moments of the last four months and a couple of days seem like such a waste of time and energy and anointing. I have a desire to preach truth to the people of First Greater Mt. Zion where Aunt Mae belonged as they rarely get the Word of God. They get more emotionalism than rhema word.

I have a sorrow for my extended family members. Tonight I realized that I come from a family of addicts- drug, alcohol, sex, jail and Jesus. No matter how prosperous I become I am nothing but a child of grace and of mercy. How is it that even in Ma-Ma Mamie's sinful mistake that she gave birth to the greatest influence on my life, my mother, who, with all the shuffling around she went through, managed to keep Christ and raise her children in the fear and admonition of God. No matter how prosperous I become I am a Grace-exception that survived the breeding ground of sin and destruction that many of my extended family occupy. This is the family I come from—addicts: men who have spent their entire lives in jail, alcoholics, men who have been raped, women who have been raped, men who have been molested, women who have been molested, adulterers, heterosexually perverse, homosexuals, pornography-watchers, number runners, number players, gamblers, illiterate and uneducated, domestically violent, booze-toting drug-peddlers, drug-abusers, HIV+, abandoned, denied, barren, physically abused, domestically abused, verbally abused, and emotionally bankrupted non-Church going and always-Church going folk. And this is just what I know.

God show me the meaning of this death. I feel as if our family has lost a level of anointing but that somehow I've been thrust into the spotlight to show what I've got.

Earlier this morning, about 12-something I had gone to bed...Moments later I just couldn't go to sleep. I thought to get up and read my WORD as I just could NOT get to sleep and I had a full day. So I was up when Asher called and said Aunt Mae died.

The Scripture I'm reading now is Psalm 90. (I can't sleep. I think I'm supposed to hear God's voice, or more, recognize God's voice in all of this.)

Lord, what meanest this experience? Why this experience in my 25th year?

"Knowledge may say that this is wrong or this is right but understanding says I know how life sometimes can make it seem like a wrong decision is right and a right one wrong."

the new gracechild

Get understanding. Understanding separates baby ministers from old, grown, Holy-spirited and wise ministers—no matter what the age. Understand the perplexities of the human heart and the choices it faces. Understand understanding. Knowledge is good—it'll make sure you don't perish. But to what will you be alive? What will be your quality of life if you lack understanding?

Knowledge may say that this is wrong or this is right but understanding goes one step further and acknowledges how life sometimes can make it seem like a wrong decision is right and a right one wrong; and then wisdom will give you the how to and the time to move in handling that which is Known as wrong or right.

Understanding is now agreement, or obeisance to that which is of the perfect will of God, of His plan. Understanding is the heart's ability to witness with and identify with another's heart's ability to be deceived and have called the deception justified.

Is there a minister in the house who has knowledge?
Is there a minister in the house who has wisdom?
Is there a minister in the house who stayed long enough in fellowship with God after the storm to hear God speak His purpose for his trial? Or a minister who has chosen to remember the meditations of her heart's journey toward purity? Or a minister who sat at the feet of what God taught him or her through his or her Jordans, wildernesses, Elims, Canaans, Mt.

Moriahs, Jerusalems, Babylons and especially Golgathas long enough to, without condemnation, tell someone in need of help, "I understand."

Until you can say "I understand," without judgment, what is the quality of your ministry? How close are you really to that line of being of Christ and how far are you really from that line of being of the Pharisees?

Is there a minister in the house?

<u>chewing gristle</u>

my father was 27 when he and my mom had me.

i am 27.

it has taken 27 years for me to realize that my dad is, has been and probably will always be my best friend.

if you reap what you *saw* then God, i need You to give me at least 27 years with my oldest son, with each son, as it may take him just as long to realize who i am and really want to be to him.

is there anything i can do now or then such that i don't have to wait as long as my dad has before his firstborn son said, "hey man, you're my best friend"?

You told me to ask my dad to be my best man years ago. in faith, i did it. in obedience, i did it. he quickly rushed, "hey man, you can ask torry or damon..." but i stood on the Word you told me to do and he was honored. but now, at the same age he was when he with You and my mom co-created me, i feel that i have found myself—both halves of myself and now the honor is mine that he would agree to stand with me.

in falling and now in standing, i found the moses sr.-manhood in me and i marvel at it and celebrate it. i had 27 years to be betwixt and between in my feelings and in my spoken and meditated realities of my father and of the perceptions of my father. now i pray, give me another 27 to stand solidly every day that my dad is my best friend.

i tell mom all the time that her love and sacrifice has always brought me to the wealthiest parts of life and of myself. what i did not know was that sunken in the wealthiest alcove of the predestined me was a man of the same name, my father. (no the II needed anymore.)

i did not know my father until i knew pain so i guess in answer to my question, if my sons are ever to know me as a best friend, i cannot hide, shield or cover all pain from their midst. if only for the one reason that i, in all sobriety, call my dad, "friend", then it was and is good for me that i have been afflicted; that i might learn Thy statutes. the statute which screams in the presence of my right-now space is, "my father and i are one. when you have seen me, you have seen my father." okay, it may not be a statute but it is a revelation, no, it is THE revelation which is john's cry in the wilderness of my personal greenehouse~ making my pathway ready for Christ to do new, never seen or heard of or imagined things in the relationship between me and my sons and me and my sons and my father.

it took the exact age dad was for me to truly esteem him higher than myself. i know You to be the God of all ages. please, in my present age, do this for me. no, do this for You. "picture it: Sicily, 2000-and-whatever", (man, I just love that show!): the opportunity to negotiate (and it always is a negotiation) and then share one piece of gristle with my dad—split between me and my sons and my brothers and their sons while in my house just being family...my mansion in heaven.

ACCT 270-10
Justification By Brokenness

11-19-00 (In-Field Training)

i never had to defend my mother.
never.
she never caused me shame. never
now her praise-that is sitting under her praise brought attention
and there *were* times when i *was* embarrassed; but embarrassment
without understanding the who, what, whys and hows of her
always then-"when?"-then praise is not embarrassment; it's a post-
dated badge of honor in the kingdom.

that's what i want. but sadly, i know only an "nth" of the who,
what, why or how of my mother's way that has never caused me
shame: brokenness. she was so broken by shame that she didn't
want that shame to be a part of her children's lives. but if I want
woman who will never cause my children shame, what is she going
through now? by what has she been leveled and shattered? i mean,
if this kind of brokenness makes a woman who should end up
"x", perpetually under and simultaneously [mounted] on the
wings of God; and this is the same level of integrity and holiness
and determination that i want to find myself one with, does it not
mean that today or yesterday or in the months of her yesteryears
that my rib, my wife, my on-sight i know "this is bone of my bone
and flesh of my flesh" has been broken?

i don't know. what i *do* know is that i have been looking for
someone who has it all together? not completely right. what i *do*

know *now* is that i, today, am looking for someone who has been broken; or who is a first or second generation of togetherness because her mom or grandmother was broken and she *understands* brokenness.

i have desires. don't get me wrong. i mean, i want her to be "BOOM! KaBLAMM! CaBOOYA!" to me, but, for the sake of my kids, i will sacrifice the "BOOM" for a woman who understands brokenness such that she desires a walk with Christ such that they never have to defend her. a woman like that is worth the wait. i mean, a woman who fears the Lord (for whatever she's had to go through), who will walk before Him such that she'll bring honor to His name and will be the glory of my life and the foundation of my children's destinies is worth how ever long it takes for me to find her.

who can find a virtuous woman?
my dad. look at my life; of my "but such *were* some of you" testimony because of his choice.
who can find a virtuous woman?
my closest college friend- my best friend whose counsel strengthens my countenance daily.
who can find a virtuous woman?
i can. (because) i now understand the beauty, the virtue of brokenness, of understanding brokenness.

Black Male Author at
His Desk Editing His Book

No more accommodations.

No more apologies for being good.

It's not arrogance I'm just through apologizing.

To do so now is against receiving the full weight of God's glory for this season of my life. And I selfishly want the full glory.

When I had a degree, 5 credits from the second, but for survival sake had to work in a mall for the same per hour wage (not even a salary) that I made ten years ago as a teenager, no one asked me to apologize.

When I had to walk everywhere because I couldn't afford to keep my car, my luxury car, on the road, no one asked me to apologize.

When I had to wear the same five suits that I have worn for the past five years and had to mix and match the same couple of shirts and ties- and the suits shined and I had to keep the jacket on because I didn't have money to take the shirt to the cleaners, no one even hinted at an apology.

When my main source of income was as a food runner in a restaurant the size of a football field and I ran food Friday nights and all day Saturdays non-stop to all tables to make ends come nigher than they did last month; and when I had to clench my teeth together and bridle my tongue while I served (and each of these adjectives were interchangeable for each ethnicity depending on the day), rude whites, demanding Blacks, arrogant Africans, condescending West Indians, linguistically speed racing Puerto Ricans, "you're smiling and nodding but I still can't understand what you are saying" Europeans, "you are giving off an air that you think you're better than me but can't eat anything on the right or left side of the menu" Middle Easterners and complaining, attitudinal, misbehaving and untrained people from all of the world with their kids running all over the place and causing all kinds of accidents~ no one even suggested that I apologize for being where I was and doing what I was.

When Orangemen and women who were a season ahead or behind me came to the restaurant and gave me their cards and asked, "So what are you doing?" and I had to respond, "This" -and there was always an immediate, awkward silence that followed...And when I had aches and pains in the pores of the bones of my feet; and wore shoes, boots, too small or the perfect size but not for the task at hand and thus "cramping to my circulation" is an understatement, it was my lot. No apology desired.

No more apologies. It's not arrogance. I am just through apologizing.

When I smiled and held back tears of humiliation as I was "this old" and had to walk up for the "unemployment prayer line" at church, when I wore the same pair of shoes to work and church and play- summer, winter, spring, fall, summer, winter, spring, fall, summer, winter-until I had holes in my soles, both of them—no one inquired for an apology.

When I had to wash my dress shirts and my dress socks and my underwear and my tube socks and my t-shirts and my jeans by hand in my bathtub and my right hand was the agitator to make sudsy water to get out stench and stains and my left hand was the delicate cycle for knitted sweaters, it was told to me, "Hey, that's life. It happens." No apology.

Days when "happily ever after" was far removed and an Amen to the present hardship ending was no where in sight; when the need for financial survival and the potential money (to be earned to survive) eclipsed common sense, family values, House boundaries, Holy reasoning, and personal integrity such that I envied the members of the congregation which gathered nightly stories below my apartment for their ability to do whatever to make a dollar. [I mean, these were the very same women-men-men, a season before (with intercessors praying for me, and me armed with my Bible, my actual license to preach and a powerful praying man of God by my side), I had gone to speak that Christ was able to save them—

before the cops ordered me off the streets.] But during those days and nights and even some Sundays when the way was not made and the creditors kept calling—even on Sundays; in those times when while looking for a job, I went through parts of the yellow pages that I never knew existed- deceiving my mind that no client would expect "that" from me. First, the enemy brought it to my mind. A week later I began contemplating and wrestling and entertaining and contemplating and wrestling and working out and configuring my life, testimony and cognitive processes to reason out–"Could I actually make myself do it...with a stranger? Female and/or male?" I'm talking about days when my vision showed so much dearth within and obscurity without that I tried to calculate what would I charge for what! Sounds crazy, even to mine own ears now, (and right behind that "crazy" is a "hallelujah!") but back through that dry season of, "God, where are you? I am drowning"—I didn't even look for an apology.

And for the years, before the sloth came in, when I had the drive to get a job in, out, or about my field and I interviewed place after place, week after week, day after day—Atlanta, Syracuse, Manhattan, Long Island, Brooklyn, Atlanta, WDC, Virginia, Maryland, Television, Radio, Computers, Administrative Assistants, Accounts Payable, Secretary, Receptionist, Segment Producer, Writing Assistant, Production Assistant, Actor, Model- five credits from being declared a Master of Media Management and already possessing a bachelorhood in understanding me as a part of a phenomenal people and in writing for television, radio and film—but I heard "We just think you're going to be bored," "Sorry. We believe you are overqualified," "Sorry, Overqualified." "Overqualified." "Are you marketing or production?" "We need you to have more experience?" "We just want a secretary and we just see you trying to be more than that!", Sorry. Sorry. I'm Sorry. We're sorry. Mrs. Ransom is sorry. Mr. Hanania is sorry. "We're sorry but although your qualifications are quite impressive, we have decided to go with another" applicant...candidate...person. Sorry Overqualified.

For the years my heart ached, "Overqualified, for what?" See, the years I was deemed overqualified to work—across the board—meant, in every other non-moemeant, I was defined as under qualified. Under qualified—across the board—to meet bills, to get out of debt, to get benefits, to get sick, to get well, to take time to rest, to buy me something, to attend Orange weddings, to attend childhood mentor funerals, to bring gifts, to tangibly celebrate others, to eat balanced, to enjoy life, to work. During these three years I have not been asked one time to apologize for being too— just to take my too somewhere else.

And for the times when for holiness and integrity sake I lived as a gypsy, out of a duffle bag and evicted a two-year-old into his parent's room and made his 5X8 room my home and a pallet on the floor was my bed; and although love was there I still crept to eat food out of someone else's refrigerator because "it just wasn't mine." And the week when my labor pains hit and I heard the enraged answer from the left, "I told you to-...I can't help you! You got yourself into this mess and it's time you took responsibility for your own actions!" and from the right, from my brother building his family, "Moses, I love you. But I'm not going to be able to allow you to stay here as long as I planned", and from home on one phone, (the response to hearing his 27-year-old son at rock bottom) "Son, do you want to come home?" and from home on another phone, (in the midst of her tears because she knew Jerusalem didn't have anything for me but also seeing the consequences of decisions I made in Babylon that had led me to the negative square root of me), "Son, living out of your car is not an option. You always can come home."

He made a way.

And now that Grace alone is bringing me to a place that I sense the "blessing that overtakes"... And now that by Grace alone I am alive to see day breaking, for me; and now that I have gone past saying purely by faith, "whatever my lot, it is well" to it really being well with my soul; and now that the prophetic, exegetic, Jerusalem-genetic and Babylon Jenkins-Kinetic have all pronounced and confirmed the Jabez Prayer blessing for my life—that "now" is my season to be blessed indeed, (to have my territory enlarged, to have God's strength, direction and means with me and to be kept from things that will be good for nothing), I live in line to be blessed completely unapologetic.

Here is what I know now: the only people who ask or expect or hint at or encourage or warrant or demand someone to apologize for being where only a Holy God has elevated him or her are people who are insecure about what they perceive that same Holy God as having done in their own lives. I've been on both sides. Trust me.

But now that I have been without in every, every, every, every, every, every, every, every arena of my life such that I can stand to be blessed, if you or you or you have a problem with it, take it up with God.

I now know what Grayson Scarborough knew at seven on the soccer field: it is okay to be good, it is okay to be great and it is okay to receive from God (and from others at times).

I have been abased. I have. Maybe not to your level of abasement but to the level of the conditions for my "well done." It is now my time to abound. It is. Maybe not to your level of aboundance but to the level of the conditions for my "well done." I will continue to miss the full weight of the splendor of God in my life in my rainy seasons if I am still feeding off and expecting others to feed off the tears from my night seasons.

No more encores

No more apologies for being good.

No more apologies for being.

It's not arrogance. I'm just through apologizing.

Double fruit sublimation: It can't hurt if you are dead to it.

14 Proverbs 8 =
23 John 12

CHAPTER 8

THE   REFLECTION'S   BIRTHDAY
PARTY   YOU CANNOT   ATTEND

3:04 pm

Happy Birthday

No exclamation point, just a mark punctuated by living.

Revelation of this last week

Last Saturday or Friday night;

I am more than nothing but a gracechild

I am an addict.

I'm still here.

Survival just means survival.

Survival doesn't necessitate living just that

"I've yet to be pronounced dead."

I occupy space.

My desk at work does that.

Rock bottom.

It's not enough to have hit rock bottom.

Every addict does that.

Jesus to John to me to you says

It is when you hit rock bottom and also die that much fruit comes forth.

If you're there, die.

Happy Birthday

No exclamation point just a mark of punctuated living.

I'm 27 now.

I've lived through life's commas gone past semi-colons and am in pain because I'm reaching back for what lies on the other side of a Divine period or maybe it's an ellipse, but whatever it is it has been Divinely punctuated as "not now."

Anyone can survive an addiction but when God restores the years the locusts have taken it is that you would live not just survive. Whether my addiction is the accommodations of my heart or the provisions for the flesh I know not—I really don't know—but what I do know is that I am broken, I am without,

I am nothing but a gracechild,

I am an addict (a special kind of addict, of my own ways)

and I am finally all YOURS.

3:24 pm

Georgetown University

MBA Office of Student Life

THE ONE SONG I STILL CAN PLAY

my life was torn beyond repair
i felt so alone seemed like no one cared
YOU came along and gave me **this** song
To ease the pain and erase the shame

YOU could have left me standing there
With no one, no one to care
YOU promised me YOU'D be there on time
And YOU did just what YOU said

Against all odds i made the choice
To give YOU my trust and now i rejoice
YOU answered my prayer not a *moemeant* too soon
YOUR words i embraced
my tears YOU erased

YOU could have left me standing there
With no one, no one to care
YOU promised me YOU'D be there on time
And YOU did just what YOU said

i gave it up
That's when YOU blessed me
i let it go
That's when YOU blessed me
Lord, YOU brought me through,
now i'm brand new

i said "have YOUR way"
That's when YOU blessed me
And stayed in the race
That's when YOU blessed me
Lord, YOU promised me YOU would hear my plea
And YOU did just what YOU said

"That's When You Blessed Me"
Words by Tony Wilkins
Recorded by the L.A. Mass Choir

LIFE SUPPORT:
the grace child's hymn

I need Thee, Oh, I need Thee E'vry hour I need Thee O bless me now my Saviour I come to Thee Oh, I need Thee, Oh, I need Thee E'vry hour I need Thee O bless me now my Saviour I come to Thee I need Thee, Oh, I need Thee E'vry hour I need Thee O bless me now my Saviour I come to Thee Oh, I need Thee, Oh, I need Thee E'vry hour I need Thee O bless me now my Saviour I come to Thee I need Thee, Oh, I need Thee E'vry hour I need Thee O bless me now my Saviour I come to Thee Oh, I need Thee, Oh, I need Thee E'vry hour I need Thee O bless me now my Saviour I come to Thee I need Thee, Oh, I need Thee E'vry hour I need Thee O bless me now my Saviour I come to Thee Oh, I need Thee, Oh, I need Thee E'vry hour I need Thee O bless me now my Saviour I come to Thee I need Thee, Oh, I need Thee E'vry hour I need Thee O bless me now my Saviour I come to Thee Oh, I need Thee, Oh, I need Thee E'vry hour I need Thee O bless me now my Saviour I come to Thee I need Thee, Oh, I need Thee E'vry hour I need Thee O bless me now my Saviour I come to Thee Oh, I need Thee, Oh, I need Thee E'vry hour I need Thee O bless me now my Saviour I come to Thee I need Thee, Oh, I need Thee E'vry hour I need Thee O bless me now my Saviour I come to Thee Oh, I need Thee, Oh, I need Thee E'vry hour I need Thee O bless me now my Saviour I come to Thee I need Thee, Oh, I need Thee E'vry hour I need Thee O bless me now my Saviour I come to Thee Oh, I need Thee, Oh, I need Thee E'vry hour I need Thee O bless me now my Saviour I come to Thee I need Thee, Oh, I need Thee E'vry hour I need Thee O bless me now my Saviour I come to Thee Oh, I need Thee, Oh, I need Thee E'vry hour I need Thee O bless me now my Saviour I come to Thee I need Thee, Oh, I need Thee E'vry hour I need Thee O bless me now my Saviour I come to TheeI need Thee, Oh, I need Thee E'vry hour I need Thee O bless me now my Saviour I come to Thee Oh, I need Thee, Oh, I need Thee E'vry hour I need Thee O bless me now my Saviour I come to Thee I need Thee, Oh, I need Thee E'vry hour I need Thee O bless me now my Saviour I come to Thee Oh, I need Thee, Oh, I need Thee E'vry hour I need Thee O bless me now my Saviour I come to Thee **Never an amen.** I need Thee, Oh, I need Thee E'vry hour I need Thee O bless me now my Saviour I come to Thee Oh, I need Thee, Oh, I need Thee E'vry hour I need Thee O bless me now my Saviour I come to Thee I need Thee, Oh, I need Thee E'vry hour I need Thee O bless me now my Saviour I come to Thee Oh, I need Thee, Oh, I need Thee E'vry hour I need Thee O bless me now my Saviour I come to TheeI need Thee, Oh, I need Thee E'vry hour I need Thee O bless me now my Saviour I come to Thee Oh, I need Thee, Oh, I need Thee E'vry hour I

acknowledgements

I T HAS been both a process and a journey. You hold in your hands something that has been in my heart for years. However, the reality of self-publishing my first book brought me through a tremendous process of exercising faith, finding finances and learning to free-fall with God daily into some aspect of the unfamiliar. Likewise, to really die to myself, "rise to my calling" (as my father would say), and become *spirit of Moses* required an intense and sometimes painful journey of reflection, introspection, acknowledgement, ownership and continual surrender. Neither of these things—the process nor the journey—could have occurred without having several significant relationships and the counsel of key people in my life.

unconditional love and acceptance to my parents, moses and betty faye greene, the treasures of ten thousand lifetimes. i thank God for you every morning. **grace, healing and God's favor** to my greenehouse siblings: i esteem you all higher than myself. d, i could not have survived life had God not scheduled a brother so close in age. you are strength to our family. danielle, through you, God makes life make sense for me. much love. alex, you are the wind bearer that keeps me mounted above the storms. 8/27/00 will forever signify that, **if only for you**, i arrived to the right place for the right time. **strength** to sharon and marion, who have always loved me. your prayers and spiritual warfare brought about greater sustained deliverance and boldness. **good success and healing** to tracy and jerome, my brothers born for adversity. my life was made rich beyond measure when God added both of you to the greenehouse. through you, i understand grace, strength and mercy. **limitless mercy and**

lovingkindness to brandon. part of my understanding what is the breadth, length, height and width of God's ways and his love towards me is because of your existence. **wisdom and internal peace** to the holliday, brown, jones, gorham, green(e), and thorne families. one of the greatest joys in my life has been being your grandson, nephew and cousin. **power, boldness, and unhindered access to the Father always** to anastasio, strauss-michael, arden, and their siblings, who continue to hang with me through every season. your childlike faith, innocence, and fervor for God daily encourages me to be transparent. i deny me because i know the best is yet to come for each of you. **love** to...true motions of agape, the hall family. thanks for calling me "son" and for extending your home, hearts and family to include me; to the late albert r. thorne. your table set the stage for my inner greatness. "see you in Heaven, man." **goodness** to my goddaughter, briana renee, a living reminder that God is a restorer. i live a more purposed life because of you.

appreciation to...elder albert l. brown, for giving me deep roots; pastor h. bernard alex **for preaching** "God led you this way because He knew you would yet give Him praise"—a **Word that freed** my understanding and strengthened my feet to stand; first lady trina jenkins, for the challenge to *never* be satisfied with where i am in Christ; prophet thomas weeks, who mightily prophesied my publishing calling into existence (over the phone); pastor tyrone stevenson, through whom God allowed me to know that every delay of 2003 was a part of His plan; dr. keith gilyard, dr. janis mayes and professor sharon hollenback, who challenged **me** to think beyond the obvious and **to grow** as a writer, intellectual and student of life; and bnme/gracechild administrative supporters cecelia, coretta, kimberly, jeneen, tonya, phelicia, kendra, and tony for lending of themselves to make this thing happen with excellence.

strength and joy to torry, who mourned with me in the ashes, interceded through the storms, and stirred me to rebuild. greater than riches is a brother who can call on the name of the Lord. thanks for **still** being here. **spiritual renewal** to eric, who strengthened my hands and ran with me in accomplishing part of the vision. this gracechild is up and "running with the horses" because of your belief in me during a critical season. i believe now in you. **peace and blessings to** jodie, rhonda, and karen, **consummate friends, prayer warriors, and women of God.** nuff said. **gentleness** to teresa yvette, eric tyler, mark anthony, sean anthony joel, and sonya, who heard it all and didn't change; and to christopher robin, the very personification of friendship. i never would have made it through the storms without your listening ear.

lovingkindness to...e.b., u.j., a.w., g.b., r.t., and w.b.—ministers of friendship. **continual intercession** to...brian, darling, doug, erica, gilda, gloria, jacqueline, kiana, maris, shirley and tex, **who gave** of yourselves when i had nothing; and dianne harmon, as i am a work in progress that made it to this level of renovation because of your **prayer** life. **love with faith** to...shirley **"ma"** berkeley and alberta mckay, who fed my soul wisdom, food and laughter i cannot repay. i know you both want me to try, but i can't (smile); the Sunday afternoon crew, who taught me how to tell a good joke; ministers linda thomas and josephine miller who kept me accountable to my words; maureen, who steadied my path; and barbara holt, a supermodel of supernatural business fortitude. thanks for your way of excellence and friendship. **joy in the Holy Ghost** to...thomas, whom t. d. jakes would describe as a strange friend. "where'd you come from?". you reminded me that i was created to win and that every pain was about the kingdom of God, not me; minister stephen hurd, thanks for believing in me from the beginning. the ministry of "it's working for your good," "be strong," and "healed (by the power of His word)" strengthened me to complete this work; sharon ewell foster, who **freed me to bleed**, and v. michael mckay for "you never gave up on me"— a song which carried me.

faith...to my georgetown mba 2002 fam—my chawla brother sam, officer pulley, lenny, jack, canet, david, monica, rob s., and all the students who always spoke investment into my potential; donnell, who reminded me that God was "only an arm-stretch away"; reuben and jerry for speaking words which **changed my reality**; thomas, who prayed in a fast for holiness that nearly took me out!; carlous, before whom i could be real; sheryl, who taught me the power of my anointing and reminded me while at the threshold what was at stake if i went back. i walk in greater integrity because you did not judge; and oprah, a portrait of Romans 8:28 who mirrored the "in spite of" determination i hope to one day see reflected in myself. **gratitude, hope and salvation to**...vickie, scott, cheryl, the brittany place family, markees and the tight 'n up posse, who always spoke of a future greatness, as if they saw the finished work of Jesus Christ already accomplished in me. **a spirit of excellence** to dr. melinda kramer and the students of my fall 2003 english courses at pgcc. i found me and unspeakable joy in serving each of you. **abundant blessings** to the intercessors of first baptist church (bay shore, ny and glenarden, md), new jerusalem baptist church (brentwood, ny), new bethany baptist church (islip, ny) and china; and to those who were stedfastly committed to spiritual warfare and prayer on behalf of the book: betty faye greene, lettie plater, veronica pierce, and brenda jordan.

i never would have made it from childhood to the present without the yoke-destroying, burden-removing music ministry of shirley caesar, dorothy love coates, james cleveland, sara jordan powell, andrae crouch, walter hawkins, tramaine hawkins, rev. clay evans, hezekiah walker, monique walker, james moore, charles woolfork, richard smallwood, fred hammond, yolanda adams, melonie daniels, kirk franklin, maurette brown-clark, cece winans, marymary, donnie mcclurkin, marvin sapp, tonex, and israel houghton. my soul is escaping the snares of the fowler, in part, because you honored the world with your musical callings and testimonies of faith. dorinda clark-cole, "*i am still here...it's by the grace of God.*" thank you for opening your soul and life experiences as a witness of the power of God. i pray the kingdom of God in its fullness for each of your lives.

double honor to evangelist rick amato, living and breathing confirmation that **God honors those who face their greatest pain**. this book is my asking God "what?" and no longer "why?". your challenge for me to see myself as a spiritual being having a humanistic experience has brought a settling to both my conscious and unconscious realities for every "why?" with which i struggled with God for many years. i finally died because of you.

lastly, to...my molesters, thank you; those whom i wounded in finding me, i'm sorry; those who are proud of me, pray for me; my Lord and Savior, i o u me, and to myself—obedience is the highest form of praise; you do you only as He calls you to do you.

ABOUT THE AUTHOR

spirit of Moses (Moses T. Alexander Greene) *is a freelance writer, English professor, model, actor, producer and events manager based in the Washington, D.C. Metro area. Steeped in the important elements of artistic expression including the visual and performing arts, his innovative writing and production track record has afforded him many positions in the communications arena, including being the Writers' Assistant of ABC's "All My Children."*

Licensed into the ministry of the Gospel of Jesus Christ at age 25, Alexander Greene often employs out-of-the-box and wildly creative means–through the venues of writing, multi-media productions, the performing arts, music ministry and the preached and taught Word of God–to bring empowerment for healing and deliverance to many. His unique skill-set coupled with a distinctive and impassioned ministry of transparency has made him a highly sought-after facilitator for arts, educational, broadcasting and ministry-based initiatives.

A native of Long Island, New York's South Shore, Moses T. Alexander Greene also serves as the Chairman & Chief Executive Officer of Bethesda Nu'ahch Ministry Enterprises, (b n ME) LLC. This company houses Gracechild Publishing and The Arden Charis Group, a consulting firm that specializes in artistic direction, ministry development and public relations.

Author's Notes

The original name for this book was, "I Never Knew I Needed To Be Washed: Prose, Poetry and My Reality." (It is now the title of a piece in this collection). The title of this book changed as I began to realize and walk in a knowledge that not only was there a need for me to understand that I *too* needed to be washed, but also an understanding of where God had to bring me to wash me. It was not in my hometown, where I was "known" and "loved." I was outsourced; stripped of all honor and brought to a land for outpatients...like me.

This book, "my proposal: nothing but a gracechild" is a collection of my typed and hand-written thoughts, journal entries, short stories and parables communicated to you as I wrote them. 'gracechild is raw. It may have misspelled words and incomplete thoughts, but during those heated, emotion-driven moments of my life, I didn't have perfectly spelled words and completely thought-out situations, I had life. Life wasn't always, but has become my responses to the inner epiphany that God is not now or was He ever waiting for me to have everything together.

One of my favorite childhood songs was, "You Don't Have To Be A Star, Baby [To Be In My Show]" by Billy Davis and Marilyn

McCoo. Even as a kid, Marilyn McCoo's part in the third verse, did something to me.

> *And I don't need a superstar,*
> *[cause] I'll accept you as you are.*
> *You won't be denied 'cause I'm satisfied*
> *With the love you have inspired*

Something powerful, almost spiritual, stirred within me every time I communicated that reality with my lips. There was a resonance of "yesdom" that I cannot put into words.

Shielded from the consequences of my actions and of others closest to me, and also belonging to a particular *class of celebration** in my scholastic and religious communities, as I matured I began to qualify and disqualify people by their "star-potential"—what I saw them to possess. (*"Class of celebration" is used to describe the "celebrity" status that enveloped my childhood as I was nurtured in a community with the title "Mr. Greene's Son" or the inquiry, "Mrs. Greene is your mother?" which always brought with it a level of prestige and admiration.)

Before the present season of my life, somewhere in the quiet place of my heart's vanity was this unknown reality: "You didn't have to be a star but you sure better have had sumthin!" This was based on my perception of myself to have been good enough; good enough for my parents, my siblings, my closest friends and somewhat, for GOD. But thanks be unto God for Washington, D.C. The District is my Babylon; my land of exile which has humbled me to an "If had not been for the Lord who was on my side" identity.

The power of the GOSPEL (the life, death, burial and resurrection of Jesus Christ) and my understanding of the hearts of the fathers of *this* prodigal son (unconditional acceptance, love, intercession, dreams deferred, hope and many tears) was made clear for me in this season of my life through some of those songs I had as a kid. Some were hymns ("I Surrender All", "Oh To Be Kept By Jesus", "Tis So Sweet to Trust In Jesus"); some were songs I heard growing up at my church on Long Island ("Oh, Lord, Keep Me" and "Farther Along") and many came from the gospel songs my mother played early Saturday mornings as she exercised or on the 8-track in her black Oldsmobile Delta '88—("He's That Kind of Friend" and "Jesus, I Love You" by the Hawkins Family, "Holy One" by Tramaine Hawkins, "Keep Me in Your Care" by James Cleveland, "Take Me Back" by Andrae Crouch, "Help Me" and "This Joy I Have" by Shirley Caesar, "I Won't Turn Back" by Sara Jordan Powell and "I'm Holding Onto My Faith" by Dorothy Love Coates). However, a few select others were straight-up, without a doubt, pop-culture, R&B love songs and songs with words of admonition and wisdom like "The Best of My Love" by the Emotions, "For The Love of You" by the Isley Brothers, "Never Knew Love Like This Before" by Stephanie Mills, "You Give Good Love" by Whitney Houston, "Waterfalls" by TLC, and "Just Because" by Anita Baker. As God was tempering my heart toward greater pliability for His usage (by way of the things I was going through by His design), both of these genres of songs—the hymns and the ones I heard on WBLS and KISS-FM in New York—*ministered* to me. That's right, I said even the words of the R&B songs ministered to me.

I <u>still</u> now and probably will forever go up into praise unto God in the spirit of my mind as the Father has repeatedly made known to my heart, even before entering this land of exile, the following reality taken from an Anita Baker classic,

> *I love you*
> *Just because*
> *I love you*
> *Just because...Just because I do...*

God loves me; period, finished, through and for all of eternity. During the first season I took note of being rejected and disqualified by man—men and women of the Church—I found the deepest meaning and the most awesome awareness of total and complete acceptance by GOD that I had ever known. What joy is now available to me as I face each day knowing that I have his love; and not for any reason, any quality that is of myself.

Reader, this book has not been published because the author has been perfect. I haven't been and I am not. But I am blameless. Because of His son's blood I am declared blameless and justified. Also, I don't need (i.e. there's no longer a hunger in me to be "superstar anything"; just to be Moses.) For such a time as this, my "chosenment" is to empower you and those closest and furthest from you with this knowledge: GOD wants you <u>as you are</u>.

This book exists to tell you that you don't need to be a superstar, just come to Him. You don't need to have your habit, your addiction or your sin under control. <u>You</u> cannot get it under control. It will take the daily aid, assistance, correction, comfort, speaking, correction, leading, more correction, empowerment and revelation of the Holy Spirit of Jehovah God for you to have victory over sin. You also don't need to be perfect or look perfect or dress perfect to come to His house (church); <u>God</u> <u>wants</u> <u>you</u> <u>as</u> <u>you</u> <u>are</u>. If a church wants you to be a superstar in order to first come to Him, that is not the liberty of the Father in operation. Be out! (Now once you get to the House and you begin to taste and to see the Lord's goodness in your life for yourself there will be an inward pressing for you to please the Father in every thing and in every way possible. It will be a work of the Spirit of God, not of man. But don't let the hows and the whats of who you are right now and what you are presently going through stop you from getting to the Heavenly Father's house. It's HIS house. Whoosh!)

So as author I won't say, "I hope you have enjoyed what you've read in this book", but rather, "I hope you have gotten understanding." Understanding always surpasses enjoyment; and it lasts a lifetime. This text was from one work-in-progress to another; from one work-in-progress to another.

And she called his name
Moses: and she said, "Because
I drew him out of the water..."

Exodus 2:10

<u>He</u> sent from above, <u>He</u> took me,
<u>He</u> drew me out of many waters.
<u>He</u> delivered me from my strong
enemy, and from them which hated
me: for they were too strong for me.

Psalm 18:16-17

Jehovah-rohi, thank You for my journey.

Deuteronomy 8:2